BREAK OUT

BREAK OUT

A CRIMINAL'S JOURNEY
TO ETERNAL FREEDOM

JED LINDSTROM

First published by Lets Go Ministry, Inc. 2015
This revised and expanded edition published by Lets Go Ministry, Inc. 2016

ISBN: 0-692-81934-7
ISBN-13: 978-0-692-81934-0

First Edition Information:
ISBN: 0-692-52690-0
ISBN-13: 978-0-692-52690-3

Printed in the United States of America

Revised and expanded edition cover design and layout by Daniel Strickland
Revised and expanded edition editing by Abigail Shirley
Writing by Larry J. Leech II from the Original Edition is included in this Revised and Expanded Edition.

DEDICATION

I want to dedicate this book to you. Yes, you the reader, and your families. I wrote this book for you to be blessed in some special way so you may be touched by the Holy Spirit and set on fire to share God's Good News with everyone you can.

My wife, Erica, and I have committed to pray daily for those who read this book. We want you to know that God loves you very much. He is able to save, heal, and deliver you from whatever you're going through.

John 17:1-5 says, "After saying all these things, Jesus looked up to heaven and said, "Father, the hour has come. Glorify your Son so he can give glory back to you. For you have given him authority over everyone. He gives eternal life to each one you have given him. And this is the way to have eternal life—to know you, the only true God, and Jesus Christ, the one you sent to earth. I brought glory to you here on earth by completing the work you gave me to do. Now, Father, bring me into the glory we shared before the world began."

PREFACE

When the idea to chronicle my story in book form was first brought to my attention in 2013, the complicated process this would require was lost on me. Little did I know how much time, energy, and help from multiple people would be needed to see it through to its final completion.

Perhaps you read the original version of *Break Out* and have picked up the second edition out of curiosity. If you're wondering why I was compelled to write a revised and expanded edition, the answer is "you"! In the months that followed the release of the first edition, many readers told me they wished the book had more context and details throughout. Although I was glad people were left wanting more rather than being overwhelmed by content, I felt the best thing to do was to listen to reader feedback and expand the original. Our prayer is that you will be strengthened in hope and faith as you read these testimonies of God's mercy, faithfulness, and power to deliver.

I want to acknowledge a number of people who have inspired me to write this book and encouraged me to never give up.

First, I want to acknowledge my Lord and Savior, Jesus Christ, for saving me and setting my feet on a firm foundation.

A special thank you to Abby Shirley and Daniel Strickland for your editing, layout, and design work on the revised and expanded edition. I also want to acknowledge the work of Larry J. Leech II on the original manuscript of *Break Out*. Writing done by Larry in the original edition is included in this expanded and revised edition.

Thank you to Mary Hart Photography for the beautiful photos you took of our newly expanded family.

Thank you to my good friend, Russell Holloway, for putting the bug in my ear to write a book and helping me to follow through with it to the end.

Thank you to my mom, Donna Lindstrom, for always praying with fervency and faithfulness for the Lord's delivering hand to break out in my life. I also want to honor my dad, Clint Lindstrom. Even though we have no relationship today, I want you to know that God loves you very much and I trust that one day our paths will cross again.

Thank you to my brothers, Chris Warmbold and Hans Lindstrom, for walking by my side through tough times and always seeing the best in me.

I want to recognize my best friend since I was three years old, Tom Anderson, for believing in me and supporting me through my addictions and struggles; Pastor Clarence St. John, a great man of God, for dedicating me to the Lord when I was one and standing with me in support of God's call upon my life; and Evangelist Jacob Damkani, for delivering the Gospel to me all the way from Tel Aviv, Israel while I was still a thief and a drug addict.

Thank you to all the police officers who arrested me and the corrections officers who watched over me while I was incarcerated. Thank you to our U.S. military who serve this nation. Thank you to the Minnesota Adult and Teen Challenge leadership and staff for your dedication to Jesus and to the broken and hurting. Thank you to Pastors Jeff and Vicki Dye for telling me like it is and Pastor Rich Scherber for telling me that I could be a world changer…and to not mess it up again!

Thank you to our staff, board of directors, volunteers, and prayer and financial partners for standing with us in the ministry by investing your time, energy, and resources.

I also want to honor the late Pat Anderson for mobilizing people to pray over every aspect of this project and agreeing with us that God's love would prevail in the readers' lives. You were a tremendous warrior for the Lord on this earth and I trust that you are rejoicing in heaven today with Jesus.

Rosella, Annabelle, Lydia, Austin, Hailey, and Ames—my wonderful children—you inspired me to write this book. For this I am humbled and blessed; thank you for being a part of my life and family.

Last, but not least, I want to honor my beautiful wife, Erica Lindstrom, for always loving me, always seeing what I cannot see, and for keeping me in line.

Jed Lindstrom
Daytona Beach, Florida
December 2016

TABLE OF CONTENTS

1. Reaching the Old Me   13

2. An Imperfect Family   17

3. Just a Matter of Time   25

4. From Bad to Worse   35

5. Looking Out for Me   43

6. Nothing Left   51

7. Beginnings of Change   57

8. Second Time Around   65

9. Training Ground   75

10. Stepping Out   95

11. Mistakes Redeemed   105

12. Brought Together   113

13. Let's Go   119

14. Restoration   129

15. The Unlikely Ones   139

Chapter 1

REACHING THE OLD ME

I watched the man approach our tent. I'd seen that walk before. The one that switches from hope to uncertainty with each step. Looking tired and unsure, he stopped a few feet away and surveyed his surroundings. I could tell he wanted to come in, but something held him back.

I stepped outside of my ministry tent, into the heat, with a bottle of water in my hand. "Thirsty?" I said, over the sound of a car zipping past us standing on the infield at the Daytona International Speedway®. He looked in my direction, still not sure what to do next. He ran a dirty hand through his unwashed hair and said, "Sure is hot out here today; unusual for this time of year."

"Yeah, it is." I handed him the bottle of water and this time he took it. "Shouldn't be this hot in February. Not much we can do about it, though. It is what it is." He twisted off the cap and took a sip.

"So what brings you my way?"

He looked around before answering, like he was unsure if he should tell me. "I've been camping with a buddy of mine." He nodded in the direction of the campground. "We've been drinking and doing drugs for the last two days. He's passed out right now; I needed to get away." I nodded while he continued. "I'm tired of being hung over and strung out. I'm sick of it. The booze. The drugs. The women. All of it. So I decided to take a walk and here I am." He dragged the toe of his boot through the dirt.

"Well, I'm glad you stopped by. You're welcome to come inside if you want. This heat is a bit much," I said as another car roared past us, drowning out my last few words.

His eyes widened. "Did you say you're the heat?"

"No," I said, chuckling and laying a hand on his shoulder. "I'm not the heat. It's hot out here. Let's go inside and chat."

He eyed the banner across the top of our tent. "Lets Go Ministry—what the hell are you guys doing here?"

"We're here to share God's love with everyone that we can."

He nodded, but didn't take a step toward the tent. "I've heard about your Jesus, but I'm not sure what to make of Him." This time the man took a long drink, almost finishing the bottle.

"I've done so many things and screwed my life up so bad that I doubt He gives a crap about me."

"Oh, I'm not so sure about that," I said. "You have no idea what I've done in my life."

He scoffed. "You? You look like you've been in church all your life and have never been in trouble."

"That's the furthest thing from the truth."

"Sure. Look at you. How could you ever understand what I've been through? You're all cleaned up with a world class smile. Nice clothes and shoes."

I gave him a quick once over before answering, not to judge, but to understand why he made the comment about my clothes and being clean. I could see why the nice clothes and shoes stood out to this guy, but I wasn't dressed much differently than him. We both wore jeans, although his were covered with patches of grease and dirt. We both wore T-shirts; his promoted a popular motorcycle brand and mine was plain white. He wore a beat up pair of cowboy boots and I wore somewhat new sneakers.

"Do you really think God cares about your clothes or is intimidated by the bad things you've done? I was sitting in a jail cell strung out on meth when He reached out to me."

He gave me a look—a suspicious, bloodshot squint with lips pursed—that I'd seen numerous times over the years since giving up drugs and alcohol for a life dedicated to Jesus Christ. I probably gave that same look to people back in the day when I was bound by my addictions. Incredulously, he said, "Come on, you? You can't possibly know what it's like to be hooked on drugs, alcohol, or both."

"Why don't we step inside and I'll share my story with you. I bet you'll be surprised."

He looked at his empty water bottle and agreed. We stepped under the cover and he asked for more water. I reached into the cooler, pulled another bottle from the ice, and handed it to him. When he finished chugging that one down, I motioned to a pair of metal chairs off to the side, away from everyone else. He nodded and followed me.

Before we reached the seats, he asked, "You really used to do meth?"

"Meth, cocaine, pills, alcohol—anything I could get my hands on," I said, taking the seat on the left so I could see the entrance. He flipped the other chair around and leaned on the back.

"I just don't picture you being an addict."

"Well," I said, putting my elbows on my knees, "Let me tell you my story and you can decide for yourself."

Chapter 2

AN IMPERFECT FAMILY

My slide into drugs, alcohol, and criminal activity started at age thirteen. I was young, getting into illegal activities at an age when many boys still want to hang out with childhood friends and see their dad as a hero. But I grew up fast and soon found myself acting and living like I was much older.

Before my descent into this lifestyle, my family was involved in church and we enjoyed a number of fun family activities together. I can remember attending the air show with my dad, canoeing on the St. Croix River, fishing at Lake Alice, and camping around Minnesota.

We attended church multiple times every week. In many ways you could say we were the typical churchgoing family—loving, friendly, and compassionate. We hosted Bible studies, movie nights, and dinner parties for church friends. But when the church family wasn't around, things got uncomfortable.

My dad was a recovering addict and my mom struggled with codependency. Mom and Dad fought. A lot. This left me sad and confused. Most of the time, I didn't understand why my parents fought. When the yelling started, I'd retreat to my room. Their fights sounded like a gong blasting in my ear. I wanted them to stop. I just wanted to have peace in my home.

I cannot remember many times when I felt loved or encouraged by my father. Dad might have thought he was being loving toward us, but much of his speech was harsh, critical, and argumentative. My mom really did show that she loved us. I could see it in her daily struggle to be a woman of God with a man who claimed the same faith, but showed no love through his actions. Mom battled to live out her faith amidst my father's unpredictable behavior.

The more I observed, the less I wanted what they preached at church or what my parents desired for my life. Too much hypocrisy, especially from my dad. His behavior tainted my view of what a true Christian should be, or at least what I thought it should look like. I didn't understand how he could appear holy when our church friends were around, but act so differently when they were not. I thought at the time, if the God we worship in church is as unbalanced and dysfunctional as our family, I don't want anything to do with God.

I'm sure my parents did their best to work out their differences. My dad hurt us with his unpredictable anger. He attempted to offset that bad behavior by doing nice things for us; another example of the hypocrisy that we lived with. He left us when I was about nine. He'd been involved in some pretty serious things for years—stalking and harassment—that finally caught up with him. He denied the charges, but investigators provided undeniable evidence. Later, as an adult, I learned more about his past and his unwillingness to humble himself. That hurt me for years, because I hoped he would come around and be the dad I always wanted.

When Mom told me Dad was gone, I wanted to celebrate. That may seem unusual to some, but when your home is full of chaos and fear, you're happy when the primary source of these problems walks out the door. As a kid, you want your dad to protect you and the family. You want him to be your hero, to show love, and be an example of how a godly man should live. For us, though, these traits weren't found in our father consistently, and when he left, I believed we were better off without him.

I wish I could say that I even loved my father at that point in my life. The truth is that I had shut him out and hated him. Sometimes a relationship gets so damaged that you lose any heart connection to the other person. As accumulated wounds of fear and rejection pile up, you try to become indifferent towards them in an attempt to bury your pain and protect yourself from future damage.

When my dad left, we lived in fear for a while because of his past. I would stay up late pacing the house and peering out the windows to make sure no one was lurking outside. The thought of him coming back to hurt my mom or us kids was constantly on my mind. Thinking about what an unpredictable person might do is very unnerving.

Then one day my younger brother, Hans, and I were playing basketball across the street from our apartment when my dad suddenly pulled up and asked me to get in his car. Hans ran home crying and freaking out because he thought I was being kidnapped. In actuality, Dad had pulled up alongside me and said, "Hop in, Son. Let's go get something to eat." I was surprised and confused because he was not supposed to be around us. Despite my fear, I got in the car and left with him. As it turns out, he wanted to get custody of me.

Deciding which parent to live with is a choice no young boy or girl should be faced with, but in my case the decision was pretty easy. There was a part of me that wanted to live with my dad, just like many boys my age would, but I knew being with him wouldn't work. I still saw the volatile man who was married to my mom. He wasn't angry or hurtful all the time, but those emotions are what I remembered the most and I didn't want to be around that.

Raising three boys and trying to dig us out of the hole my dad put us in kept Mom plenty busy. She wasn't stable at the time, as one might expect after living in an abusive marriage for thirteen years. She slid backwards in her faith and disengaged from her friends. We quit attending church. We turned our backs on God and transitioned into survival mode. On the outside, things didn't look too bad. She was hurting, though, and had to push through many troubles.

Mom did the best she could, but we still ended up on welfare and lived in government housing. At the time, she had no other option. However, my mom took advantage of the opportunity she received and made the decision to work even harder. She ended up landing a great job that led to a long-term career. Mom also went back to school and graduated with her college degree. The impact of seeing this woman who was physically, spiritually, and emotionally abused not only survive, but move forward in life, never left me. Watching her inspired me to work hard and never give up.

Sports were my passion and I wanted to be on the field or at the court, but I knew my mother needed help around the house. Whether it was true or not, I felt burdened to be the dad after my father left, which was a heavy weight to carry for a ten-year-old. I wasn't equipped or mature enough to fill the void in our fatherless home; nor had I even begun to deal with my own pain and anger.

My older half-brother, Chris, who is three years my senior, spent a lot of time up north with his father. He saw the dysfunction in the family, so worked a lot and hung out with his friends. However, when he was around, Chris and I were close and enjoyed fishing, biking, and playing games together. One time we attempted to go on a bike camping trip, but my chain kept falling off and I was so tired that he had to keep stopping to wait for me. We finally made it to our destination, but it started raining and Mom had to come get us, as so often moms do when their sons bite off more than they can chew and need rescuing.

Chris and I had many good times, but as I got older and involved in drugs and crime, there were times where unbeknownst to him, I put both of us in dangerous situations. Chris joined the military at an early age to get away and do something positive with his life. I can't say that I blame him for wanting to go in a different direction. He has done very well for himself and has a wonderful family today.

From left: Jed's brother Hans, Jed, & Jed's brother Chris

Despite some of the positive times I spent with my mom and brothers growing up, I was still restless and craved attention. I didn't purposefully set out to get in trouble, but I started having regular behavioral issues at school. Most days one of my teachers would send me to the hallway for disturbing the class. I also made weekly visits to the principal's office. I spent so much in time there that it felt like they created a space just for me.

One of my elementary school teachers talked with my mom and recommended I be put on medication. Mom wondered why it was necessary. She felt I should be challenged more, not medicated. Not knowing where to turn for help, Mom allowed the school to send me to the University of Minnesota, where a number of kids my age were being tested for mental health disorders.

In addition to the mental health testing, I was also placed in groups for anger management and family relationships. I remember opening up and feeling better in some of the groups, but I was still very lost and confused. Looking back, it's easy to see that hurt and pain were the main causes of my disruptive behavior in school. I was a young man full of fear and anger. It wasn't that I just wanted to be bad or was completely unwilling to change; I felt lost and didn't know what steps to take or who I could trust. I wanted to maintain at least a sense of control even though my life felt like it was a disaster. I learned how to manipulate people by telling them what they wanted to hear.

While at the University of Minnesota, I was diagnosed with ADHD and possible Tourette's Syndrome. Doctors went on to prescribe many different combinations of medications over the decade that followed, but none of them were very effective in treating my conditions. After a while, doctors were puzzled as to what to give me. They couldn't find a mix of drugs that completely relieved the symptoms. Some worked to a certain degree, but mostly they just helped me escape from reality.

Eventually, the desire to escape—the desire to just feel good—grew increasingly strong inside of me. My dream up to this point had been to play professional baseball or football. I loved the Vikings and the Twins, who won a championship in 1987 when I was just six years old, and again in 1991. I wanted to be the next Robert Smith or Kirby Puckett. I fantasized about scoring the winning touchdown for the Vikings in the Super Bowl or hitting the World Series clinching homer for the Twins. Until one day when I was walking home from baseball practice with my cleats slung over one shoulder and my glove tucked under my arm.

Chapter 3

JUST A MATTER OF TIME

Walking home from baseball practice was common for me, and this day wasn't unlike any other. Sometimes I would stop to hang out at a friend's apartment that was on my regular route. This apartment was known as a destination for kids to get high and engage in other activities they shouldn't. Even though I had been around all this many times, drugs and alcohol just didn't hold the same appeal to me that they did to some of my friends. But that day, as I stood there looking up at the apartment, I started to contemplate what using might be like.

It's an all-too-common scenario. Kids that have had goals, dreams, and healthy hobbies for years are suddenly faced with the temptation to throw it all away. Very few addicts and alcoholics that I have encountered over the years imagined what would become of their lives after they took that first hit or drink. Whether it's boredom, trauma, or some other reason that leads an individual to consider going down this road, every user has experienced a moment where they thought drugs or alcohol were a reasonable solution, or even a good idea, to cope with life. In that moment you don't comprehend the potential cost or envision yourself giving up on lifelong dreams within a matter of weeks.

My dream to be a professional baseball player was fueled because I was pretty good at it. Even though I was a left-hander, my coaches often put me at positions typically reserved for right-handers, such as shortstop or second base. I was also a very good wrestler and point guard in basketball. I wasn't the greatest at football, but I played. I loved hockey, but we couldn't afford it. Obviously, sports were my passion, but that day, staring up at the apartment, for reasons that still aren't perfectly clear to me, I decided in my heart to lay down my dream to play baseball in order to pursue the drug life.

It took a little while for me to actually dive in and use drugs for the first time, but my mind was made up and it was only a matter of time. One day I decided to lie to my mom about staying at a friend's house so I could go get high with some friends. I smoked marijuana for the first time and my life changed forever in that moment.

It was the middle of winter—Minnesota winter—and I wandered outside all high and passed out. One of my friends found me later with my head buried in a snow bank. I remember my head being numb. I could have been seriously injured or even died the very first time I got high if my friend hadn't found me quickly. I was fourteen years old. You would think this incident might have caused me to rethink my decision to pursue this lifestyle, but nothing could be further from the truth.

After that first time, if I wasn't playing ball, I was getting high and partying. I still loved to play ball. I often went into the city to make phone calls and knock on doors to get people to play pickup games. As a kid, that was my first priority, and I wouldn't have imagined anything becoming more important to me. Ultimately, splitting time between my two favorite pastimes became too much to handle. My performance on the field deteriorated until I eventually stopped playing altogether so I could focus on getting high.

Mom knew I was starting to get into trouble. She took away privileges. She sat me down and explained the dangers of this lifestyle. I didn't listen. She grounded me numerous times, but at night I'd climb out of my window to hang out with friends. My heart was set on rebellion and no amount of love or discipline was going to change that.

Jed as a young teenager around the time he started using drugs and alcohol

My heart quickly started to harden. Built up hurt and hatred, along with the lure of the criminal lifestyle, combined to squeeze most of the love right out of me. It doesn't take long for you to become seriously corrupted and start doing things you never would have imagined. I was still going to school, but I was running around on the streets, where I started to get involved in heavier drugs—cocaine, pills, and crystal meth.

I supplied my habits by stealing and dealing to other youths and adults. I became a hardcore thief, breaking into homes and businesses. I would steal jewelry, cash, you name it; I even stole guns and sold them to gang members. Stealing served the purpose of funding my drug habit, but it also became an addiction. The thrill that came with doing the crimes was just as intoxicating to me as the chemicals. I was completely in bondage to drugs and had become a kleptomaniac. Just like when I played sports, I dove all in. I don't do anything halfway.

I started to sell drugs to the young and old, rich and poor, to families; I wasn't partial to anyone. One minute I would sell to a homeless guy and an hour later I'd be in a million-dollar home selling to a mom and dad. Addiction crosses every barrier and no segment of society is immune from its destructive power.

At fifteen, I felt like I owned the world. You pretty much could say that I was running a business. We had a crew of guys who had the reputation that you didn't mess with us. Our small crew was down for whatever and we were willing to lay down our lives for one another. We were the type of crew that if someone messed with us, we'd retaliate through robbery, burglary, giving someone drugs that were laced, or might even hurt them or their families. You just didn't mess with us. We were tight and we had money. A lethal combination.

I had more money than I ever thought I would have. While I dealt drugs, I also worked part-time. It was a thrilling time for me, because I was getting high every day and selling out of the business where I worked. Crazy thing is, I never got caught. Not once. Not even at school. By this time, the only reason I attended school was to sell drugs. The administrators knew I was an addict and was dealing hardcore drugs, but I never got busted. I really didn't even care about getting caught. I was like, come and get me. That's how my mindset was back then.

Some people think addicts are stupid. We're not. Addicts learn how to behave covertly to stay ahead of the game. They often become very sophisticated liars and manipulators, weaving elaborate stories when needed to get themselves out of trouble or to convince those who care about them to keep bailing them out. My teachers were never able to catch me with drugs and they couldn't kick me out of school because I was coming every day.

People wondered how I could possibly have gotten my diploma. It's only by God's grace that I graduated. One teacher in particular went out of her way to help me. I believe she saw something in me that I didn't and she knew there was still hope for my life. Most people didn't have any such hope for me and who could blame them? I was voted by my class as the most likely to spend the rest of their life in prison.

I was determined to get by. I wasn't one of those guys who liked to sit home all day and get high; I was more independent and driven. While some sat at home, I was out hustling to get mine. I still got high, but didn't spend every minute of every day getting messed up. The money was too good and the rush of the fast life consumed me.

Most days I would sleep till the middle of the afternoon and be up all night selling dope. I'd get up and get high right away, whether I was home or crashed at someone else's place. Then I'd meet the guys who drove in from the city to supply what we needed to deal that day. We'd take care of any business we had, such as selling them a gun, maybe a well-conditioned 9mm with a clip for $100 to $150.

After I bought coke, marijuana, pills, whatever, from the guys in the city, we'd get it ready to sell. My phone would blow up all night from people who wanted drugs. I sold to kids eleven or twelve years old, sometimes buying for their parents. That's one of the saddest things I would encounter; parents putting their kids at risk for the sake of their addictions. Of course, I was no better and really didn't care that I was the one supplying the dope. I also sold to people sixty or seventy years old. Now I have remorse. Back then, I didn't. It's not something that you really think about when you're pushing dope throughout a community. You're just thinking about the money, the next deal, or the street cred you're building.

I look back now and realize the craziness, especially at a young age. Sometimes I'd carry around thousands of dollars. What I didn't carry, I'd stash in different places. My little brother, who unfortunately followed in my footsteps, ripped me off a few times. I carried sometimes; usually the guns I stole. I also walked around with brass knuckles, large knives, and the like. I was a little paranoid. I slept many nights with a weapon under my pillow. We believed that we were safe, but if you know the street life, you know your life can change in a heartbeat. We were very protective of each other. If my crew wasn't safe, I wasn't safe, and vice versa.

Despite pushing that much dope and making that kind of money, we never joined a gang. We could have. We had enough interactions with a number of them that it would have been easy to join forces with one. With just a handful of us, we'd meet and make decisions together. I did have a lot of influence in the group, but not to the point that guys would blindly follow me wherever I went. I was a criminal and drug addict—we all were—so it's easy to understand that we only trusted each other to a certain point.

Everything we did revolved around the drugs, the girls, and the parties. We didn't really need a leader. We all wanted the same thing. To belong. That was our biggest deal. We were all wounded individuals. When you're trying desperately to cover up your own pain, you often damage others in the process. We didn't really care. We were ruining people's lives and families. Later, it wears on you, but at the time, when you're in it, you harden your heart and just don't care who is in the way.

I was fifteen the first time a gun was pulled on me. Two buddies and I were set up. We showed up to make a deal, but the other guys pulled a gun and put it to my head. They took all of our drugs, money, and jewelry. Our first thought was to retaliate, but we couldn't. They were bigger than us. When you get jacked, you have to figure out a way to cover the stolen drugs and money. We recouped our losses by targeting innocent people for money or set up other dealers who were more vulnerable and weak.

Certainly not a glamorous lifestyle, but that's how one survives—taking and being taken from. It's a vicious cycle. Surviving being robbed at gunpoint was like a badge of honor to me. After that incident, I didn't worry as much when faced with dangerous situations. There were plenty more to follow. My heart grew harder and I became more careful in my dealings as the amount of money and drugs continued to increase. The more you have, the more risk you take.

One night when I was sixteen, I overdosed in my mom's living room. I snuck my friend in and we started to do cocaine. At this point, I had already been on a bender, so hadn't slept for several days. I ended up passing out and actually dying on the couch. My spirit came out of my body and I remember looking down at myself in terror thinking my life was over. Then I sensed something behind me.

A huge, bright angel that stood from the floor to the ceiling grabbed me and said, "Your life is not over yet, Jed. You have much more to live for. You will live." Then, like a rushing wind, I went back into my body. I opened my eyes, took a huge gasp of air, and Mom was standing over me. In a panic, I flushed the drugs I had on me. Crazily, after taking a day off or so to sober up, I went right back out there and re-upped.

Mom found my drugs a few times. Mounds of it, actually. But she never got rid of it. Because she was a former addict, she knew the consequences if she did. I would have been in serious trouble with my dealers if I came up short. Instead, she confronted me. We argued with yelling, slamming doors, and lashing out. Sometimes she would show up and try to catch me and my buddies doing something wrong.

By this time, I only stayed home about half the time. The other nights I'd stay with a friend or just roam the streets all night. Either with my buddies or someone I just met, we looked for valuables to take, houses to break into, and cars to steal;

anything we could turn into money. When you get more money, you buy more dope. This expands your circle of friends.

I wasn't a big-time crook, but I was trying to climb the ladder.

Chapter 4

FROM BAD TO WORSE

I watched my classmates celebrate all around me in their caps and gowns. There was a palpable excitement in the air as these 18-year-olds talked loudly with friends and family about their impending launch into adulthood. Strung out from a four-day cocaine binge, I nervously pondered my mom's promise that she was going to kick me out after graduation day. I was trying to brace myself for this reality and convince everyone that I didn't care if she followed through with the threat. Deep down I really did care and knew I wasn't ready to be out on my own.

Life took a turn for the worse after I graduated from high school in 1998. I spent all night partying, and within a couple of days, my mom followed through on her promise to kick me out of the house. I can only imagine the fear and pain Mom dealt with in making this decision. She knew I wasn't ready to change and allowing me to stay at her house wouldn't have put any pressure on me to stop. Having a front row seat to watch a loved one destroy their life is almost unbearable.

Many parents of addicts and alcoholics eventually come to a crossroads. You can let your adult child keep staying with you or you can give them a push into reality by taking away their soft place to land. The truth is that there is no perfect solution in this situation. If you enable them, they will probably keep using indefinitely, but if you cut them off from your food, shelter, and financial support, they might die. This fear is absolutely realistic, because many addicts do die in their addiction. Any parent trying to navigate this almost unthinkable decision desperately needs continual support from friends and loved ones so the fear doesn't completely consume their life.

Mom handed me a black garbage bag to pack up my clothes. Alone in my new bedroom, I cried as I unpacked my belongings. Now that I would be living full-time in a drug house, I knew things were going to get much worse. Even though I would be living with friends and was now completely uninhibited from living the destructive life I had become so addicted to, there was fear in my heart about what the future held for me. Despite any apprehension I felt, I chose to get myself in even deeper.

I got mixed up with some pretty heavy characters and things got crazier. I was trying to move up in the world and be more than just a petty dealer. Instead of making hundreds of dollars in deals every day, I started having days where thousands were going through my hands. That may not seem like a lot, but I wasn't one of those guys making regular thousand-dollar deals. I was more of a street hustler.

Soon after graduation, I was doing $300 worth of cocaine a day. That was between three-and-a-half to four grams at the time. Doing that much about five times a week would come to almost $80,000 a year. Just in coke. That total didn't include all the marijuana I smoked, all the alcohol I drank, or all the pills I swallowed.

I thought about quitting drugs a couple of times; usually when a friend died or I was so sick that I wanted to die. When someone you know straightens up, overdoses, gets sent to prison, or is murdered, it makes you think about the lifestyle. But the pull, the adrenaline, is much too strong. For some people it takes a lot more than a friend getting murdered to give up drugs. You're somehow able to put the incident out of mind and convince yourself it won't happen to you.

I did stop a handful of times, but only for a little while. Again, the pull was too intense. For someone who hasn't been addicted to drugs, the best comparison is the need to breathe. An addict often doesn't care about sleep or food; they live only for the next bump, the next high.

Getting arrested wasn't enough for me to give up the lifestyle either. My first arrest was pretty stupid, and probably the craziest thing I ever did. I attended a party at the home of a wealthy friend. Her father worked for the Bureau of Criminal Apprehension. That night was wild. So many drugs. People were everywhere throughout the house. Some were drinking. Others were doing drugs. People were having sex in just about every room.

I was all hopped up on cocaine and went looking for alcohol. I knew her dad was a drinker. I searched the house and ended up in the master bedroom, where I rifled through the dresser drawers. In one, I found a pistol. At the time, I was a feeling a little depressed. I grabbed the gun and everything that went with it.

When I put the gun in my waistband, I had a bad feeling about how things would turn out. Most people who have been involved with drugs will tell you they had moments in their addiction where they just knew they were crossing the line with a decision they were about to make. Sure, addicts make bad choices every day, but there are some that come with a real sense of dread. This was one of those moments in my life. But I took the gun anyway. I left, stole a car, and disappeared for two days.

The Bureau of Criminal Apprehension and Gang Strike Task Force found me at a friend's house. While on the run, I got high and became paranoid that everyone was out to get me. That was pretty intense. Being chased can be quite the high for a crook and drug dealer. I deemed that high greater than the drugs I sold or used. To me, it was all part of the game of the street life. But it also can be exhausting.

I crashed on a couch in the basement of a friend's house. While I slept, the authorities surrounded the place and brought in portable floodlights. At 4:00 am, I awoke to a strange noise and peeked out the window. In moments like this, a person doesn't think; instinct tells you to get out and run as fast as you can. I bolted out the back door. A group of armed men rushed me and dragged me down the steps.

I was thrown in the back of a cruiser and taken to the police station. A cop put me in a room, like they do to criminals on television, and interrogated me until after daybreak about the whereabouts of the gun, bullets, and other stuff I stole. I didn't have the gun, though. I had thrown it in the St. Croix River in Stillwater, Minnesota.

Later, I found out that during their hunt for me, the cops knocked down twelve doors of homes that belonged to my family and friends. Two friends from Virginia were arrested because evidence relating to the gun and agent's badge was found in their vehicle. I didn't want them to get into trouble, so I took the cops to the river to recover the gun.

After my arrest on felony charges for stealing the gun, I claimed mental instability. People knew I was trying to get off easy. And I was. I won't deny that. A doctor then diagnosed me with bipolar disorder. Many addicts know how to mimic mental health symptoms in order to manipulate people. The system is setup in Minnesota to try and help those who are battling mental health issues, which is important, but that also makes it somewhat susceptible to abuse. I knew I'd receive some type of treatment, and I did, but I really wasn't honest or ready for recovery yet. Looking back, I believe a part of me was crying out for help before I really wanted it.

The second time, I got busted for invading a home. I scoped out this other dealer who was known to keep significant amounts of cash and drugs. I cased the place the night before and assumed nobody was home. Carrying only a knife, I broke in through the side door. I went through all five rooms, taking valuables, money, bags of marijuana, and drug paraphernalia. I decided to take a break in the house, so I lit up a bong and smoked it until I was high. While chilling on a couch upstairs, I heard a noise coming from downstairs.

I went to investigate and discovered someone at the top of the stairs. I kicked them back down, ran from the house, hopped into my car, and sped off. I went to a friend's house where we'd been hanging out the past few weeks. It didn't take long for the police to track me down. The cops broke through the front door and found me hiding in a closet. I was shaking, my adrenaline through the roof.

I still had the knife on me when the cops searched me. This could have resulted in a first-degree burglary charge. Instead, I was given a third-degree charge because no one could prove whether my intent with the knife was to use it as a weapon against someone or only use it to break in. Thank goodness only the one guy came into the house. I honestly don't know what would have happened to me or what I would have done if a group of guys had shown up.

My third and fourth arrests were for possession of methamphetamines with intent to sell. Warrants were out for my arrest both times when I got picked up. One of the times the police found me at a hotel. I pushed the arresting officer when he tried to cuff me. I fought five cops at once until one of them used a Taser on me.

The other time I was bagging dope at home when cops entered. I went flying out the door as per my usual attempt to flee. An officer stood on the porch and I kicked him into a snow bank. I thrived on that adrenaline. Like the other times, my escape was foiled. The cops needed just fifteen minutes or so to catch me.

An officer shoved me in the back of his car. Usually, I sat in silence or lashed out by punching things because I didn't want to go to jail. A person thinks a lot when they are sitting in the back of a police car. I usually thought about my mom or brothers. On this occasion, I cried for the first time in a long while. Another officer, one I knew from previous run-ins, asked if I thought I'd ever change. I don't know what made him ask me this, but it touched me to know someone in his position still cared despite all that I had put the police through.

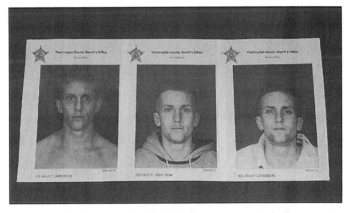

Jed's inmate photos from left to right:
Washington County, Minnesota 1999, 2000, 2001.

People who work in law enforcement or corrections are sometimes viewed as hardhearted individuals who thrive on busting and punishing people. I believe that very few actually take pleasure in watching others destroy their lives and having to daily witness the heartbreaking situations families are going through. So often these situations are the result of out of control substance abuse. Most of the people I met during my jail stints were there because of crimes that centered around using drugs or trying to get money to buy drugs. For some of us, getting thrown in jail saved our lives and was the needed impetus for change. My day would eventually come, but there were still depths of misery I was yet to explore.

Chapter 5

LOOKING OUT FOR ME

After years of accumulated experiences with seemingly random people walking up to me and saying exactly what I needed to hear in the moment, I started to think that God might be trying to get my attention. This may not seem that compelling at first blush, but when you have strangers coming up to you—a person that most normal folks wouldn't want to associate with—to offer love, prayer, and encouragement, it's unsettling. These people had no reason to talk to characters like me apart from the love of God compelling them to reach out. Although I was running from God and still not ready to surrender, the weight of these loving encounters began to chip away at my resistance over time.

People reached out to me at the most inopportune times. I'd

be about to get high or in the middle of doing something illegal, and there they would be. Back then, I wouldn't have gone to any church service or Christian event, but people faithfully invited me to them. Some may feel these were random acts, but I don't believe that. God sent those people to me. He does that. I've seen it happen multiple times. Even though I tried my hardest to act like I didn't care, the people who told me about God's love and how He was calling me impacted my life deeply.

My first encounter with one of these people was in the late 90s. I was at a park on school grounds across the street from my apartment complex in Stillwater. My buddies and I would go there to smoke weed when we could. We noticed a guy wearing a cowboy hat walking down the hill toward us.

One of the guys said, "Put it out, put it out."

I said, "No, who cares." That's how I was back then.

When he got closer, we did put out our joints. He came right up to us. "What are you up to?"

He knew. The park was known as a place where kids hung out to smoke. I think he came by that day to minister to people.

He asked us our names and I lied about mine as I laughed at him.

He looked at me and said, "I know you think this is funny, but God has a purpose for your life and that is serious."

He asked if he could pray with us and we let him. God deposited something supernaturally in me that day. This man had a word of knowledge and wisdom that struck me. In that moment, I knew God had sent him. This guy had appeared out of nowhere and ministered powerfully to us. That blew my mind.

Another time, in 1999, I'd been up three or four straight days using drugs. I decided to go to work anyways at a local office supply store in Stillwater. I was assigned to work the floor instead of my regular spot of shipping and receiving.

Early in my shift, three older people approached me in one of the aisles. The bearded man asked, "Could you help me find a pen please. Just one." I took him to the appropriate aisle. He kneeled and pointed to the pen. "Can I have one of the pens from here? I don't want the whole package; I just need one."

"I cannot sell you just one pen. You need to buy the whole pack."

He stared at me, his gaze seeing something deep inside. "You are a very honest young man. What do you do for fun, outside of this work here?"

Nobody had referred to me as *honest* in years. That one little word pricked my heart. I had a wad of cash in my pocket that I'd stolen from someone earlier that day. I thanked him and added, "I like to write and draw and kind of do whatever passes the time."

He introduced himself as Jacob Damkani. We talked for forty minutes. My manager never bothered us, nor did any customers interrupt us. Jacob told me about his life and talked about Jesus. He prayed with me there in the store to give my heart to Christ and asked for the Holy Spirit to fill me. Before he left, Jacob invited me to church and gave me the book *Why Me?*. Although I didn't go to church after that or immediately follow through on the commitment I had made to Jesus, something did start to change in me that day and I had a desire to serve God.

Jacob had wandered into the store that day at the urging of the Holy Spirit. The way he reached me and the location where he reached me didn't matter. What mattered was that God's heart was so for me that He sent someone completely out of the realm of anyone whom I would have normally listened to. Seven years after this encounter, I learned that Jacob is an evangelist from Israel. To think that God would send a Jewish evangelist from Tel Aviv to minister to a meth addict in an American office supply store is mind-boggling. This encounter set the tone for the five years of brokenness that were to follow and eventually lead me to a full surrender of my life.

Jed and Jacob Damkani are reunited in Tel Aviv, Israel
more than a decade after their first encounter

I landed in multiple treatment centers over the course of my use—outpatient, inpatient, and long-term recovery. My stays were court-ordered and usually pretty intense. Doctors and counselors tried just about everything to get me healthy and sober. They used acupuncture, Chinese patches, yoga, music therapy, group therapy, you name it, to get a person off the drugs and into a life of recovery. Some people are able to go into treatment one time and never use again, but this wasn't the case for me.

During my first five stints in treatment, I attended a number of rehabilitative meetings and sessions dealing with addiction. It's not that going to these wasn't helpful, but they rarely went deep enough to get at the root causes of my life-controlling problems. I also attended Alcoholics Anonymous® and Narcotics Anonymous® meetings. I did not take those meetings as seriously as I should have, so didn't get much out of them. Many people who attend these meetings have found them extremely helpful to their recovery, but I was not invested.

I graduated from all of the programs I was admitted to, but usually went back to using, selling, and stealing within a few weeks. The programs didn't have a component that dealt with the sin issue I battled, nor did they help me to see what God saw in me. I needed deliverance from a real Devil who hated me and desperately needed an encounter with the God who was lovingly revealing Himself to me throughout all my rebellion. My heart was crying out for something real, something fixed, to cling to.

Most of my life I had my own agenda. I usually rehabbed to appease the courts. Going to these facilities either lightened my sentence or kept me out of jail altogether. I attended a lot, and I mean a lot, of meetings. I said and did whatever I needed to get out of trouble. I was a pretty good liar. You need to be to keep your story intact.

A lot of times when I went to court, I'd admit to everything. That was the best thing that ever happened. At the time, I was genuine about wanting help. Unfortunately, the pull toward drugs and crime was greater than my commitment to get free. People who have used understand this. No matter how much you want to change, and no matter how hard you try to change, that pull, that need to get high just eats away at you until you use again.

When a person hits the bubble, snorts a line, pops a pill, or smokes dope, they shift into what I call "Superman Mode." Nothing else matters. That person feels as if they have the power of the man with the red cape. That is until the person crashes. Confused. Hopeless. Physically sick. That's how I felt when coming down. The crash is one of the worst experiences a person can have.

It's sad when a person keeps relapsing, because it damages the individual and is another blow, another disappointment, to the person's loved ones. A lot of people were pulling for me. They would call me all the time to make sure I was okay. Every time I said yes, but the pain, the ache, grew each day. My mom cheered me on. I had all kinds of help. There was no reason that I couldn't do well. I just didn't want to give up the drugs or the lifestyle. I was so thickheaded and hardhearted. I didn't want to leave it behind badly enough. That's really what it came down to.

Looking back, I believe if I had surrendered my life to the Lord earlier, I wouldn't have had to go through some of these things. So much happens over the course of a day in that lifestyle that it's hard to comprehend for a person who hasn't lived in that way. Every day is filled with danger. What was normal for us would freak out most law-abiding citizens. Crazy stuff. Overdoses and blackouts. Getting caught in a crossfire. Paranoia. Running from the police and other dealers.

During the summer of 2004 in East Saint Paul, Minnesota, I almost got myself killed. I spent a couple of months helping to sell dope out of a friend's house, gaining trust by making moves and doing dirt. During that process, I met a lot of other dealers, some of whom would try to rob us. Many nights we were so paranoid that we would sit by each door with guns waiting for someone to try and break in.

One day I was entrusted to watch the house during a slow time. I knew there were safes with valuables, as well as drugs and guns in the attic. Understandably, the house was a burglary target, and while I was there alone, two men unexpectedly came by. They knew my track record and asked if I'd be willing to turn a blind eye for some dope. I obliged and went in the other room to get high so they could take whatever they wanted.

A truck full of guys soon pulled up. They came inside and swept the house clean of drugs and valuables. Not long after they left, my friend returned and was livid when he learned what happened. I told him that I couldn't stop the men when they showed up to rob him. He trusted me enough to believe my story at the time, but two days later, it all came crashing down after he had investigated the incident further.

Nervously, I sat on the couch in my friend's house lost in thought waiting for the truth to come out. *Why did I do this for a little dope*, I asked myself, *how could I be stupid enough to think I'd get away with it?*

A car door slammed and jarred me out of my daze. Two men wearing black gloves appeared before me. This was it. I felt like a deer cornered by a pack of wolves. The men had a friend of mine in their grasp who had also been involved with the burglary. They grabbed me by the back of my shirt and escorted the two of us to the basement where they put an AK-47 to my mouth and a crossbow to his. This was it. We were hopeless. There was nowhere to run. No one could hear us scream for help. We were ready to die.

All of a sudden, as they were interrogating us, my friend's phone rang. A power I didn't recognize at the time swept through the room. He somehow managed to answer before they could get the phone away from him and he revealed our location to the caller. God supernaturally disarmed those guys right before my eyes. With their cover blown, our captors temporarily left the basement without further harming us. I believe someone was praying and He delivered us from death.

He sent out his word and healed them, snatching them from the door of death. Let them praise the LORD for his great love and for the wonderful things he has done for them. Psalm 107:20-21

We were kept in that basement for the next week or so, drugged and held like hostages. Eventually, they decided what we had done wasn't worth keeping us any longer or killing us over, so they let us go.

This experience brought me so close to death, but also revealed God's presence in my life once again. I would soon personally encounter the One who is greater than all.

Chapter 6

NOTHING LEFT

Wandering the streets with nowhere to go and nobody left to call who trusted or wanted me around, I began to realize that I had slipped into total desperation. No longer did I feel like I owned the world. No longer did I have a tight-knit crew or thousands of dollars going through my hands. It was just me. Alone. Homeless.

At the start of this game, I never imagined this could happen to me. I was too smart, too clever, too good at hustling, too good a thief to ever really have my back against the wall...or so I thought in the beginning. Eventually, you've screwed so many people over and burned so many bridges that it all comes crashing in on you. Sometimes it only takes one choice and one person more powerful than you to cut you down to size. My life was almost taken from me, and now, that's all I had left.

An incredible sense of despair and loneliness overshadowed me. Friends didn't want me in their cars because they knew the cops were after me. Family didn't want me in their houses because they knew I was an unmitigated thief. People looked at me with resignation, seeming to accept the fact that I would die an addict. It felt like everyone had given up on me, but thoughts still flooded my mind of times when my mom would pray for me after the cops brought me home as a teenager and young adult. The love Mom carried, combined with the power of her prayers, was an unstoppable force. Those memories helped me in the darkest times.

It was quite a shock when the rain started pouring down on me while sleeping on a park bench and I realized there was no roof over my head anymore. I had nowhere to go; no place to call my own. And yet something inside me still said everything would be okay if I could just find a way to get high. I can't think of a clearer picture of the bondage drug addiction brings. Here I was, having destroyed my life to the point where I had nothing left, and all I could think about was getting my next fix.

People are trapped in the drug lifestyle. Yes, there are choices to make and every addict has to make a decision at some point to either stop using or die in their addiction. But the trap is devastating. The hopelessness that you feel when you realize you'll do anything for the drug, you'll pay any cost, and you are fully in its grasp, is suffocating. Eventually, you start to believe that it's too late, and one way or another, the drug is going to kill you.

One of the cruelest ironies of addiction is that it makes you incredibly self-absorbed and incredibly self-loathing at the same time. You're so driven by your desire to get high that you'll trample on anybody—parents, siblings, friends—to get your hands on the dope. But simultaneously, many addicts experience intense feelings of remorse, rejection, and regret. You lose vision for your life and get used to disappointing people. The unrelenting compulsion to use coupled with accumulated regret and pain sometimes lead people to take their own lives. I certainly contemplated suicide several times as the fierce oppression closed in on me.

There is a battle that rages over the lives of addicts and their families. Evil is real. The Devil is real and bent on destroying people. Addiction is one of the primary methods he uses. People get hooked, and when it's not fun anymore, they may try to stop using, but have to fight against their own desires and demonic opposition.

One time when I was incarcerated, a Mexican gangster from Chicago who had turned his life over to Jesus gave me this scripture at a Bible study:

A final word: Be strong in the Lord and in his mighty power. Put on all of God's armor so that you will be able to stand firm against all strategies of the devil. For we are not fighting against flesh-and-blood enemies, but against evil rulers and authorities of the unseen world, against mighty powers in this dark world, and against evil spirits in the heavenly places. Ephesians 6:10-12

Trying to speak into my life, he said, "Jed, this is a spiritual battle and you have to see it that way to really understand life."

That night I stayed up till 2:00 am and then woke up early.

"Did you take time to read that scripture?"

"Yeah, I read it."

"I prayed for you till 2:00 this morning, Jed."

That had been the exact time I fell asleep. This encounter was significant because this man helped me to understand there was more going on than what I could see. I believe God sent him so my eyes could be opened to the raging spiritual battle that was going on all around me.

I am so thankful that I had a praying mom who would not let me go. Between the abuse I subjected my body to and the dangerous situations I put myself in, I easily could have died out there. The power of God is real and active. If you are crying out to God for an addicted loved one right now and are growing weary, don't give up! They desperately need your prayers for divine protection and for the Lord to awaken them to His call and vision for their life.

God continued to show up, protecting and providing enough to keep me alive, but still desperate. I slept in parks, dug through bins of donated clothing, and had to scrape funds together just to buy a donut and cup of coffee. Sometimes I would stink because I'd go a week between showers. One time a family found me sleeping along the road and put me on their front porch so I was safe. Other times, someone would walk by me and just share a kind word or a laugh. I'm sure this probably didn't feel like a big deal to the person at the time, but these small acts of compassion gave me a glimmer of hope that I still had value. It may sound trite, but never underestimate the power of reaching out to people in the simplest of ways. God can use anything.

The weight of my desperate circumstances began to break me. I was dealing with plenty of hurt when I started using drugs, and now I had heaped ten years of destructive choices on top of that. My pain started coming out in every direction. I would roam around neighborhoods wondering if anyone would care for me. I'd walk by homes and see kids playing with a parent, especially a dad, and yearn for what they had. I was the crazy looking person on the sidewalk yelling at the air. You know, the type of guy that people will cross the street to avoid walking by. Yeah, I was that guy sometimes. A mess.

Half out of my mind and fearing that I was seriously physically ill, I turned to a childhood friend. Remember the apartment I was looking up at wondering about getting high for the first time? It belonged to this friend's family. Ten years later, I asked her to take me in. Even though I got my start in drugs at her childhood home, she was a true friend to me, and one that I knew I could reach out to. She and her boyfriend gave me a place to stay, but knew I needed help.

My friend was not a churchgoer, but remembered that in the past, the only times I seemed to have any hope were when I was trying to seek God. Not knowing what to do with me exactly, they brought me to church on Sunday. Clinging to the glass meth pipe I had in my pocket, I went forward for communion. It's these parts of my story that cause me to marvel at the grace and compassion of God. He didn't strike me down for being irreverent or scold me for not cleaning myself up before coming to Him. I had to have been one of the most disheveled characters to ever stand at the front of the church. But His presence was sweet to me at that altar and filled me with hope, even as I stood there in my brokenness, ignorance, and uncertainty.

I began having deep and meaningful conversations with my friends in the days that followed this experience. I felt sick and truly believed that there was some type of serious disease in my body. There is intense paranoia and anxiety that goes hand-in-hand with coming down from these types of drugs. The mental anguish, combined with the realization that I had been abusing my body for so long, led me to believe that I must be dying.

My fear of death and my hope that God might actually desire a relationship with me started to provide motivation towards change. Who was this God that would be kind enough to reach out to an addict in his most desperate state? What could He possibly want with my life? Even the faintest hope that my life still had meaning and purpose was something I was clinging to in that moment.

But there were still natural consequences to consider. I was a wanted man by police. Prison time was the likely outcome if I were to come clean. My options were jail or back to the streets. But how much longer could I really last? Everything finally boiled down to this one decision.

I called Mom. I'm sure she figured I was just after a warm meal or money like I'd been so many times before.

Chapter 7

BEGINNINGS OF CHANGE

"Mom, I wanna turn myself in. Can you come get me?"

For the past week or so, I had been calling my mom every couple of days to check in. She knew something was up with me. I was despondent and just not myself. Mom always had plenty to worry about with me, but lately my level of desperation had gotten so severe that she wasn't sure if I'd make it through. She must have been shocked to receive this phone call from me.

Mom showed up to take me to the Ramsey County Law Enforcement Center. I got in the car before I could change my mind and asked to make a stop for cigarettes. Inside the gas station bathroom, I destroyed and threw away my meth and weed pipes. Nervously, I bought a pack of cigarettes and started chain smoking as we made the 30-minute drive to the detention center. *Am I really going to go through with this?* I asked myself. Even though I knew this was my best option, the thought of turning myself over to police was completely unnatural to me.

The car ride was intense. Mom was praying out loud and pleading with me, "You're my son. I want you to live!"

We pulled up to the door and Mom looked at me as if to say, go on now, it's time to finally put an end to ten years of madness for the both of us. We said our goodbyes and I drug my 100-pound frame slowly up to the entrance. Nothing but skin and bones, dressed in dirty jeans and t-shirt, I walked into the lobby looking like death warmed over.

"I'm here to turn myself in," I said to the man at the desk. He looked up at me and said, "Have a seat—it'll probably be forty-five minutes or so till we can book you."

What a perfect opportunity for an addict. It certainly wouldn't have been the first time for me to run away from my problems. But this time, I didn't. Perhaps it was the combination of God's grace, my mom fervently praying in the car on her way home, and a determination I now felt to see it through that kept me from running. Whatever the exact reasons were, I had a sudden resolve within me to stay put no matter what.

I can just imagine what I looked like sitting on the detention center steps, franticly sucking down cigarette after cigarette. It wasn't my finest moment, but at least I had a desire to do something right and felt the will to follow through for the first time in a long while. It felt good to want to do right, but unusual.

Those forty-five minutes felt like hours, but at last my name was called.

Time to go through the normal booking routine of fingerprinting, strip searching, and showering with an officer close enough to reach out and touch. At least I was clean for once. No drugs on me anymore. No stench from running the streets for days on end without showering. I put on my jailhouse oranges and was escorted to a cell.

"How are you feeling, Jed?" asked an officer who stopped by my holding cell, "Do you think you're a danger to yourself or others?"

"I don't know. Maybe. I'd be lying if I said I didn't want to hurt people sometimes...or myself. I'm not sure I have much to live for anymore."

"I'll pretend that I didn't hear that."

If the officer was operating by the book, I would have been placed on suicide watch in a cell with nothing but a toilet and bare bed. I think he was able to read into my statements enough to see that I wasn't really a danger to anyone. I was just a listless young man trying to figure out what to do with myself.

Sitting on the edge of my vinyl jail bed, I began asking myself, *How did I get here? How did I go from being a 14-year-old kid wondering about smoking a little pot to a 24-year-old homeless drug addict with multiple felonies?*

What I needed to do suddenly became clear to me. I knelt down on that cold jail cell floor and begged God to spare my life. I knew if I didn't change I'd die this way.

I sat crying for a long time, until I shivered from the cold of the floor. At first, I didn't say or think much. Eventually, I mumbled, "God, fill me up." I repeated that over and over.

My words became more desperate. I cried out, "Change me! I don't want to live like this!"

I sensed something stirring deep inside me. A yearning to really change replaced my half-hearted desire to be different. I felt a strong sense that what I actually needed was *to be changed* rather than change myself. For years I had some desire to change, but never the strength or willpower to see it through. I was missing the power of God to transform me at the deepest level.

I called out to Jesus and gave my life completely to Him. There was no agenda, no thought, no plan in my mind at that moment except total surrender. It was October 11, 2004.

In my cell, I experienced the real feeling of a person wrapping their arms around me. I knew it was God, even with my limited knowledge of faith. He held me for a long time. I relaxed in the peace that seeped into my being. As I let go in His presence, the pain and hatred started losing their grip on me. The love and tenderness of God the Father started to restore my soul even in those first moments of relationship with Him.

I grabbed a Bible someone had left in the cell. After years of people telling me about God, I sought Him earnestly for the first time. I happened upon Ephesians 4:28. Part of this verse reads, "thieves steal no longer". I thought to myself, *I can't ever steal again?* Oftentimes, people chuckle when I tell them this part of my story, but this was a real revelation to me. I was the guy that you didn't want knowing where you lived because I was such a thief. Living an honest life was a concept lost on me.

After experiencing His salvation, presence, and Word all in this one encounter, I asked God to fill me with His Holy Spirit. I began praying in tongues soon after. I didn't have much understanding or theological knowledge at this point. There was nothing in my mind or background to cause me to doubt this experience. The evidence of the genuineness of the encounter was very real.

His Word started to come alive to me. I didn't know which scriptures to read. Most times I just flipped open the Bible and read random passages. Most say this isn't the way to read it, but God divinely took me to the words He wanted me to read and it was all brand new to me anyways. I spent a lot of time in the Word. My heart continued to change as the Holy Spirit opened my eyes to the truths it contained.

People noticed the change in me right away. My whole countenance was brighter and the hardness dissipated. I could even feel the difference physically. It felt like I had been completely broken down mentally, emotionally, and physically and was now being rebuilt by the hand of God.

I don't think people realize how bound up they are until they've been loosened by the power of God. Many peoples' emotional issues affect their bodies with tense shoulders, backs, or stomachs. When the Holy Spirit touches those areas, He brings freedom and the person can move freely. I believe this happened to me. And I've seen it with many others.

I let go of insecurities, pain, guilt, and unforgiveness that I had been holding onto for years. Some people have described this feeling as a physical weight leaving their body, like a heavy rock falling off their shoulder. For me, the experience was more of an emotional breaking, followed by healing. I love that about God. He liberates people who are bound by the enemy.

Some of my old buddies from the outside ended up in my unit, where the jail kept forty to eighty of us. Most of them got word about the change in me and wanted to see if it was real. When we hung out, I talked about God's work in my life. I didn't judge them, but I did have an impact. I could see that. I hoped they would believe the change in me and accept that God loved them too. I wanted them to have a life-changing encounter. I know God used me to speak into their lives, but a lot of times, people don't want to hear truth from someone who used to run with them. It wasn't my place to change them. I just tried to plant seeds like so many had done for me.

It's understandable why some of these guys doubted that my change would stick. I had certainly gotten clean in jail before only to relapse when I got out of treatment. There was nothing in my history with these guys that would cause them to assume it was real. But this time it actually was. I didn't give my life to Jesus because I was in a jail cell. I truly surrendered my whole life to the lordship and love of Jesus.

You have a lot of time to think in jail. Sitting there for hours, then days, then weeks and months, causes you to remember different people from your past. One of those people for me was my childhood friend, Tommy. As kids, we called each other daily, biked to school, and played sports. On weekends we stayed up all night, laughing and playing. Unsure why he popped into my mind, I wrote and told him everything that had happened and asked for his forgiveness. To my surprise, he wrote back. He forgave me. Better than that, he wrote that he believed I had changed. This confirmed what I'd experienced. My change was not a figment of my imagination. I needed others to love and forgive me for my wrongs towards them. And they did.

Every day something broke inside me. Over time, I felt more remorse about the ungodly things I did. The lies. The anger. The deceit. The manipulation. I had inflicted a lot of pain. Friends, family, strangers, and the community were all affected by my actions. I would soon find myself in a courtroom answering for some of them.

Because of my three prior felony convictions, I faced a guideline sentence of thirty-three months in prison. I sat on the edge of my thin mattress waiting to be taken in front of the judge. Random thoughts tumbled through my mind. I didn't focus on any particular thing. I just spaced out. Once in a while, I remembered the words my mother spoke during our drive to the jail, "You're my son. I want you to live."

My mom and I had endured a tenuous relationship at times with frequent arguing. Usually I was the instigator. But she never gave up on me or stopped praying for me. I finally realized she was just trying to love me! I'm convinced the Holy Spirit used her relentless love to stop me from going on the run many times. His intervention in my life became more and more clear as I looked back.

Going before the judge is usually unnerving, but this time, a peace surrounded me that I barely understood. I looked and felt so much different this time around. Despite the change in me and peace that I felt, I was still a little nervous that the judge would hold to the guideline sentence.

Hardened criminals, people without remorse, and desperate addicts stand before judges every day in courtrooms around the country. Many of these people, including myself in times past, swear up and down that it will be different this time if they could just get another chance. Those who work in the judicial system are bombarded by the grim realities of recidivism almost continuously. It's hard to blame judges if they get a bit jaded and cynical over time. Witnessing repeated failure tends to do that to a person.

There I was in front of the judge. Another failure. He looked at me almost with a sense of disbelief that these words were going to come out of his mouth and said, "I don't know why, but I will have mercy. If you are interested, I will send you back to Minnesota Adult & Teen Challenge."

It's a shocking feeling when someone has pure, unadulterated mercy on you. Especially when that person has no good reason to believe they should be merciful. The judge didn't seem convinced about the decision, and yet, he was compelled to make it. I believe the judge saw a broken man before him. Even if he didn't know it, I had been radically changed by the power of the Holy Spirit. Jesus was all over my life. I knew God had intervened on my behalf.

Chapter 8

SECOND TIME AROUND

I stepped up to the desk to retrieve my belongings from the officer. A comb, lighter, pack of cigarettes, and dirty outfit completed the list of my possessions. Nothing like starting out fresh without a dime to your name or even a decent pair of pants. Upon my previous releases from jail, finding someone to rob so I could reestablish myself in the drug game was my first priority. Not this time. I walked out of jail that day in November 2004 knowing this would be my last incarceration if I remained faithful.

Mom smiled as I made my way to her car. There was an excitement in her eyes, a joy in believing that this time would be different. The ride from jail to Teen Challenge was much more pleasant than our previous trip together.

I discovered a suitcase full of new clothes, toiletries, and other necessities in the car. I have a wonderful mother! If you've ever been to treatment before, you know there's usually a list of *bring this, don't bring that*. In her excitement, Mom went out and purchased everything on that list. The gesture meant so much to me. That suitcase of brand new items—little things like deodorant and underwear—was symbolic to me of the fresh start I was embarking upon.

We pulled up to the door of the center in South Minneapolis. I handed over my cigarettes and lighter before getting out. They wouldn't do me much good in a tobacco-free, Christian recovery program. Regardless, I had no desire to ever smoke again. We parked and Mom walked me up to the admissions office where we embraced and said our goodbyes.

I was admitted to the *Restoration Program* for graduates. One of the realities of recovery is relapse. That is not to say that everyone who enters recovery relapses at some point. I know plenty of people who never touched a substance again after completing the program. In my case, I didn't take it very seriously the first time and wasn't ready to completely surrender my life. Others have had major life transformations in the program and are very serious about sobriety, but the pressures of life and temptation led them to pick back up again. Whatever the case, I am so grateful that Minnesota Adult & Teen Challenge provided a place for me to return to.

One of the first stops I made upon my return to Teen Challenge was in Pastor Terry Francis' office, the men's program director. "Come in, Jed. It's good to have you back. Let's talk about what your program is going to look like. I want you to start in Level One."

"But I've already done Level One," I protested.

There I was, trying to run my own program right out of the gate. This is a common problem for people going through treatment. Even sincere ones are tempted to try and run the show. It's an attempt at maintaining some type of control even though you have lived completely out of control for a long time.

I'm sure Pastor Terry could see my desire to be in charge right away. Through a broad, knowing smile he said, "The chemical dependency curriculum will be good for you."

This was a bit of a rude awakening. For a few weeks I had been living in a state of spiritual euphoria, capped off by an amazingly favorable trip to court. Suddenly, I was confronted by the fact that this was going to be difficult. Yes, God had started an incredible work in my heart, but it was far from being complete. I needed to humble myself, dig in, and do whatever it took to do it right this time. Even if it meant starting over at square one.

I decided to go to my classes with joy and press in hard. A desire to do things with excellence rose up within me. You have never seen such immaculate toilets as the ones I was charged with cleaning. We had work detail four days per week and I decided to sweep, dust, and scrub harder than anyone else. You would have felt very comfortable doing your business on my floor. Cleanest bathrooms in any treatment program guaranteed.

Beyond our regular chores and afternoon cleaning, Teen Challenge also provided us with opportunities to volunteer at community events and serve people outside of the organization. We were able to provide moving services to individuals. It's kind of ironic to have a group of criminals and addicts hauling other people's valuables around. But we did it, and I don't think anything went missing!

The most significant service opportunity was participating in choir. Everyone was a part of the group that traveled around Minnesota to sing and give testimonies in churches. Picture seventy-five recovering addicts—some of whom had been clean for just days or weeks—performing at your church on a Sunday morning. We were a motley crew and lacked formal training, but God used us powerfully to minister hope to people. The act of sharing your testimony with a large group of strangers is difficult, but can also be very healing.

My heart needed a lot of healing. I did not fully recognize how damaged I was. Over the years, I had wanted a relationship with my father, but my attempts to develop one always failed. Thankfully, I had a wise counselor at Teen Challenge who was able to shed light on how the broken relationship with my dad impacted my view of God. I didn't even realize what abandonment meant or that my deep-seated feelings of rejection could badly skew my perspective of Him.

My counselor asked, "Jed, do you think the lack of relationship with your dad affects the way you view God?"

"I don't know," I said, "I haven't really thought about it before."

"Do you think you could tell God all the things you would like to tell your father?"

"I don't think so. If I said everything to God that I want to say to my father…"

"What, you think He can't take it or something?" my counselor challenged me, "You think He can't handle blatant honesty or a little cussing?"

"You want me to cuss at God?"

"No, Jed, I want you to be real with God and pour your heart out to Him. I guarantee that He can take it."

That night, I did it. I approached God with reverence, but also with a sense that it was safe to ask Him my questions.

I cried out, "Why did I have to go through this pain?"

"Why the rejection and abandonment?"

"Why did my father give up his parental rights when I was just a boy?"

"Where were you when my family was being torn apart?!"

On and on I went, pouring out the questions I had tried to suppress for so many years with drugs. Finally, everything was on the table. I left no stone unturned in my heart. My counselor was right. God could handle me being real with Him. After all, He already knew every unspoken thought and intention of my heart. There was nothing I could say to shock Him.

Once this encounter took place, I was able to start relating to God as Father. Before this, I knew that Jesus was my Savior, but to think of God as a Father? That was a foreign concept to me. Grasping this was the starting point for working through the effects of being abandoned by my earthly father. I still had questions, but a revolution had begun in my heart against the lies that I was unworthy and unwanted.

Fathers should be a source of security and protection to their children, but when they walk out of the picture, a deep sense of insecurity can form. Why would my dad leave? Wasn't I good enough? Important enough? Worthy of his affection and love? These questions about one's value and worthiness can continue to haunt a person, so when I was told that I could relate to God as "Father", that brought up a very skewed image in my mind. I had to learn what a real father is through reading scripture. The Bible revealed to me that God is a faithful defender, comforter, and provider to His children. He is not distant and will not leave me.

As I started to understand that God was a good Father who desired a deep relationship with me, things began to shift in my life. Slowly, I began to reach my hand out to Him, trusting that He would not abandon me. In this place of relationship, God began to deal with the unforgiveness I was holding onto towards my dad. Working through this was foundational and necessary if I wanted to be right with God. One of the most black and white statements that Jesus ever made has to do with forgiveness:

> *If you forgive those who sin against you, your heavenly Father will forgive you. But if you refuse to forgive others, your Father will not forgive your sins.* Matthew 6:14-15

Forgiving someone doesn't mean you condone their actions. It doesn't mean that God condones their actions either. But we must choose to extend forgiveness to those who have injured us in the same way Christ forgave us. When we forgive, it doesn't mean that all of our relationships will be instantly transformed or that everything works out perfectly. To this day, I am not in relationship with my earthly father and this is very painful to me. Forgiveness is something that we must continue to walk out by God's grace. It is not merely a one-time event.

I learned that God had extended mercy to me in even more poignant ways than I first realized. I discovered through discussions with staff members that many had been praying for me in the months leading up to me turning myself in. Teen Challenge hosts alumni events and I decided to go to one the summer of 2004 to see if I could manipulate people to give me money (I don't recommend trying to scam a bunch of former addicts). People saw how terrible I looked and knew I was in serious trouble. It was then that the prayers started in earnest.

As I replayed some of the significant events in my life from that time period with a particular staff member, we made a remarkable discovery. I told him about the week I was held captive in the basement and he distinctively remembered that he was praying for me throughout that time. My life was truly in jeopardy and this faithful intercessor was praying for me all along. This confirmed to me that the Lord kept His hand of protection over my life throughout the most dangerous of circumstances I put myself in. My level of trust in God's goodness continued to deepen as I learned more and more how He had kept me safe.

In addition to God keeping me safe through these years, He also strengthened my family to not write me off. My mom and brother had every reason to want nothing to do with me anymore. They chose to remain in relationship with me and continued to hope things would change one day. My brother followed in my footsteps of using drugs for a few years himself. Mom had to deal with the pain and fear that comes with having two addicted sons. Both of us had plenty of restitution to make to our mother.

Holiday passes were part of the program for those of us who were in good standing. For the first time in years, I was prepared to have a sober Christmas with my family. Mom picked me up from Teen Challenge for the multiday visit I would be spending at her house. There, my brother, Mom, and I sat around the tree like a *normal* family.

Our big gift to Mom that year, other than being sober, was to come clean. We confessed that we had stolen her jewelry and other valuables over the years. We asked for her forgiveness, which unsurprisingly, she gave without reservation.

Mom handed me a nicely wrapped package. The thousand-dollar mobile phone bill that I had racked up in her name was inside. Staring up at me in big, bold letters across the top of the bill was "PAID IN FULL". I had felt led to start paying this debt to my mom off soon after I got to Teen Challenge. I made it one payment into this process when Mom decided to wipe my slate clean. She had faith that the changes in my life were going to stick. What an encouragement this was to me.

My mom was and continues to be a testimony to the power of mercy. If she could forgive us and my dad for the things we had done, certainly I could keep walking through the challenges of extending mercy to those who had wronged me. Many people in my Mom's position would have become bitter over the years, but she continued to trust in God and keep a soft heart.

That Christmas break was a pivotal time for my family. Real healing began to take place among the three of us. When all you've known is turmoil and strife for years, it is amazing to experience restoration and peace. More work was still needed, but it felt good to have everything in the open. I was able to return with a renewed sense of purpose for the rest of my program.

Jed's mom, Donna; Jed; Hans' daughter; and Hans in 2006

Not long after returning from break, I felt led to start getting up early in the morning for prayer. I started to wake up at 5:00 am every day. As time passed, I began leading other students who would join with me to seek God in a little upstairs prayer room. We encountered Him powerfully during these times. It was as if the Lord came down to personally meet with us. We were brand new in our faith and there was a desperation to seek Him. There was no other alternative for us. Either we would be healed, set free, and transformed by God, or we would end up back in our old lives.

After leading these morning prayer times for a short while, I had a dream one night. I was driving around in a small silver car with a trunk full of Bibles. I went up and down the back roads, highways, and dirt roads of the United States. Everywhere I went, I was handing out the Bibles to people. I had no idea what the dream meant, so I told a staff member about it. He encouraged me to take this dream before the Lord in prayer. I followed his advice and then didn't think about it much for quite some time.

I already had a sense that I was being called into a life of ministry before these things started happening. Having my fellow students look to me for spiritual leadership and the car dream served to solidify this sense. I couldn't imagine going into a regular vocation, but also had no idea what doing *ministry* really looked like. This dilemma plagued several of us in the program. We had a passion for the things of God and desired to be active in bringing the Gospel outside the walls of Teen Challenge. But we weren't equipped to do so yet.

In Teen Challenge, you sit through classes and services almost every day of the week. I wasn't expecting a sudden answer to my dilemma during my normal routine. One day, a senior leader visited our morning prayer time and brought the most amazing news. He had recently visited a Teen Challenge Ministry Institute for graduates in another state and brought back the recommendation to start one in Minnesota. The local leadership team agreed and made plans to quickly open an institute of their own. The one- or two-year program for graduates would offer safe, sober housing and ministry training. Because of the urgency our leadership felt to open the institute, it would be ready in time for my graduation in June of 2005.

Chapter 9

TRAINING GROUND

Eight months ago I was sitting in a jail cell and now I'm surrounded by a bunch of people who are far smarter than me. I must be crazy for thinking I can study the Bible. I've never read a book all the way through in my entire life! Who do I think I am?

My excitement about the ministry institute quickly turned to intimidation when I got there. They piled books and assignments on me. Suddenly I found myself in groups debating theology with people who seemed intellectually superior. Truthfully, we were all very green that early on, but some of my fellow students presented much better than me. Even though I felt inferior at times, I knew that I was supposed to attend the institute. It was a battle during the first few months to get my bearings.

I began to study the Bible in depth for the first time. Truths contained in God's Word that I didn't even know existed before came alive to me. The areas of skepticism I held regarding Christianity diminished as I delved into deeper theology and apologetics. It's possible to have such a powerful encounter with God that you know deeply it is real, but your mind can still grapple with aspects of your newfound faith. Finding answers to many of my questions strengthened my convictions immensely.

Although I was learning a lot of new information, I was struggling to keep up with my classes. On top of that, continuing to work through anger, unforgiveness, and insecurity added additional challenges. Things had become very real in my life. The Restoration Program had been difficult at times, but now I was trying to simultaneously build on the progress I had made there with my personal issues and do loads of schoolwork.

For a while towards the beginning, I thought I might get the boot from ministry school because of my failure to pass enough classes. I was still pretty dysfunctional in handling life and relationships. I didn't know how to manage my time very well or be responsible for deadlines. Rather than fully completing assigned reading, I would skim small sections and pray that God would help me to pass the classes. I wasted time engaging in heated theological discussions with classmates even though my knowledge was very limited. I would have been much better off investing that time in my homework!

Somehow I managed to stumble through my first quarter despite all of these issues. The leaders of the institute must have known that I needed to be there, because on paper, they had reason enough to kick me out. Even though they weren't threatening to do so, I was struggling hard to keep going. I wondered if there was a different path for me. Perhaps I could just find a job and try to get by. In my heart I knew God had called me to the institute, but it didn't make sense to stick around and keep failing. Something needed to change.

As I turned to God in desperate prayer, He quickly revealed that the needed change was in my heart. The problem wasn't the reading, the assignments, or my classmates. I was the problem. His presence was very tangible during this encounter and He spoke directly to my heart. Yes, I needed to study harder in order to pass my classes, but I also needed to seek Him daily. He was after my heart and wanted to prepare me for my life's mission to reach *the old me*. It was time to stop debating, wasting time, and worrying about things I couldn't control. It was time to get serious about the call on my life. His call.

Just a week or so after I had this encounter with God, the ministry institute underwent a significant shift. When you launch something brand new, inevitably there are growing pains and tweaks needed along the way. In the institute's case, the decision was made that more attention needed to be given to hands on training. Up to that point, the focus had mainly been on academics and deepening your personal devotional life. Those elements would remain critical components, but now students would also be charged with doing ministry projects.

I thrived under the new model. Not only were the classes more manageable for me, but I was also able to put my creativity to use in forming outreach opportunities. All my life I have been action oriented. There is something inside of me that shouts, "GO!" Being released to start hands on ministry work under the guidance of seasoned leadership was the beginning of a crazy new adventure that continues to this day.

My first ministry project was working at a 24/7 Christian call center. For several months, two fellow students—Abby and Heather—and I worked a weekly shift at the center. You never knew what to expect when picking up the phone. One time it could be a suicidal individual desperately reaching out for help and the next time it could be someone calling because they wanted to receive Christ. We prayed with people for healing, deliverance, provision, for their addicted loved ones, and every other type of need a person could have. The three of us had only been Christians for about a year, but we all had powerful testimonies of transformation in our lives.

Volunteering at the call center forced us to rely on God's direction. During this season, I began to learn how to hear His voice and minister to people going through difficult times, just as so many others had done for me. Now it was my turn to help people through their struggles. This training would prove critical for my next steps. I didn't know when I started this project that I would soon find myself going to another level of hands on ministry.

Some classmates were planning to take a trip to the International House of Prayer in Kansas City over the 2005 Christmas break. I wasn't very interested in making the journey for their 4-day conference at the end of the year. After all, who wants to drive 400 miles down icy Interstate 35 in the dead of winter for extended days of worship and prayer? A bunch of Teen Challenge graduates, of course. Regardless of what I was feeling about it at the time, I decided to make the trip with my fellow students. I had no idea what God had in store for me.

After spending four days in the prayer room and conference sessions, the Lord spoke clearly to me. At 11:45 pm on New Year's

Eve, just when the conference was peaking and people were getting ready to celebrate, I heard, "I want you to leave. Go out and share My love with everyone you meet. This is how I want you to finish this year and begin the new one."

On my way out the door, I bumped into a classmate who wanted to come with me. The company was more than welcome. At least there would be two of us jumping into the unknown together. I knew little about evangelism at the time. Less than one hundred feet out the door of the massive conference center, a man jumped out of a bush and scared me half to death. Still a little stunned I asked, "What are you doing?!"

"I'm hungry," he said.

At that point, I did the first thing that came to mind. I gave him $5.00 for a sandwich and told him that Jesus had totally changed my life. He smelled really bad, so I offered to bring him up to my room so he could take a shower. He wasn't interested.

Sensing that this man living in a bush had real potential, I asked him, "What's stopping you from becoming the next Donald Trump?" I'm not sure where that came from, but I kept thinking how much God loved him and that his life didn't have to end on the streets, poor and dirty. Not that God looked down on his humble circumstances, but I just felt like there was so much more for him.

The encounter was positive overall, but no dramatic miracle or conversion. I shared the Gospel, my testimony, and tried to take care of some physical needs. Oftentimes, this is all you can do. You can't force *results*. You share the love of God any way possible and trust Him to do something with your weak words.

My night wasn't over yet. Turning the corner, I witnessed a guy dressed in all black wearing batting gloves. Instinctively, I knew what he was up to. I said to him, "Hey man, going to batting practice?"

"I don't play baseball."

"I know. Name's Jed—can I talk to you for a minute?"

He listened as I shared my testimony with him. A car passed us for the third time. Knowing someone was trying to pick him up I said, "This night will not end well for you if you do what I think you're about to do."

He shot me a knowing smile and said, "Thank you."

At that point, the man left. I have no idea what he did after that. For all I know, he rendezvoused with his buddy and still committed the robbery or whatever crime they were up to. But maybe he didn't. Regardless, I believe the Lord used me to warn that man. It doesn't mean that he made the right choice. We just have to be obedient to share the material He gives us. People still have to make their own decisions.

The man in the bush and the man in black were my very first street evangelism encounters. I'm sure I didn't sound polished. I know I didn't have all the answers. None of that really mattered. That night I learned what God can do with a simple person who is willing to reach out. The results weren't profound. Were they supposed to be? I didn't know one way or the other at this point, but I went back to school refreshed.

I began to find my niche as I progressed through the second half of my first year of ministry school. I started discovering a love for people. After my shifts at the call center, I would go back to my room at the institute and pray for the individuals who had called in that night. There was a passion ignited in my heart for seeing people come to Christ. I wanted them to experience the same freedom I had been given.

Opportunities slowly began to open up for me to give my testimony publicly. I found myself sharing at the Salvation Army and a few small local churches. It was definitely raw content. I was used to giving testimonies from my time in the Teen Challenge Choir, but my content now started to expand. I began passionately charging people to share the Gospel with the lost; it just poured out of me. All of a sudden, God had birthed a message in my heart that desperately needed to be shared.

Unwittingly, a friend asked me to attend a ministry's dinner one night, not knowing what an impact the event would have on my life. This particular ministry focuses on giving free Bibles away. I was impressed by the work they were doing, so I volunteered to be a courier, receiving and handing out Bibles. In addition to getting this new assignment, that night I met a woman who introduced me to a life-changing organization.

At this point in my Christian walk, I didn't realize ministries existed that focused almost entirely on evangelism. The woman I met introduced me to a Minneapolis based group that went out twice a week, every week, to do street ministry. My only experience was the Kansas City encounters. Unsure of exactly what evangelism looked like when done by people who knew what they were doing, I decided to check it out. It also seemed like it would be a great avenue for giving away the Bibles. This would prove to be a fateful decision.

For the duration of my ministry school experience, I participated in street outreaches every Friday and Saturday night. Even though I was still fairly new in my faith and had some apprehension, I stepped out, trusting that God could use me in some way to touch lives. There was a part of me that felt right at home on the streets from the start. I wasn't a polished minister of the Gospel, but I already sensed that my calling was to missions and outreach.

In my quest for learning the best way to do evangelism, I studied pretty much every technique out there and tried them out on people. Those poor people. Set methods were not my forte. Don't get me wrong, there are good principles to be gleaned from studying different evangelism methods, but I had a hard time fully implementing them. To me it felt unnatural leading a person through a canned approach. It seemed like the best experiences I had ministering on the streets were when I was personal, sincere, and spontaneous. I wondered if I was just being naïve. Maybe my off-the-cuff style was wrong.

Sitting in prayer before an outreach one evening, something finally dawned on me. I thought, *Why am I trying to be somebody else?* From that point on, I stopped worrying about methodology and started focusing on sharing God's love with simplicity in the ways He was leading me with each person. Just being kind, real, and expressing the joy I had inside gave me the opportunity to minister to people in an impactful way. The Gospel message doesn't need to be overcomplicated.

I was amazed how the Lord started opening people's hearts during these simple encounters. The more I shared my faith, the more I felt my desperate need for God. Burning inside me was a desire to really know Him and be able to share a living faith about a living God. I didn't want to be out there trying to convince people to follow a religious figure who died 2,000 years ago; I wanted to share about the resurrected Christ and see His Spirit move in power! My walk needed to have life so I could minister effectively. I didn't *feel* on fire or see amazing results every day, but I wanted to know that the message was alive in my heart every day.

You never know when a simple prayer time will change your life forever. Preparing to go on the streets one night to minister, I suddenly had a vision. A metal train flashed by my eyes like a blur. I explained the vision to a friend who was with me and asked, "What do you think it means?"

"Have you ever been to New York City?"

"No, I've barely left Minnesota. New York City—what made you think of that?"

"I don't know. First thing that came to mind. I've been there and have friends that live out there. Would you ever consider going?"

"Probably not. I'm on probation. I don't think my PO would let me go to New York. Cool vision, though."

Thinking that might be the end of the vision, I dropped it. But for the next three days, I couldn't stop thinking about what the vision might mean. I wondered if my probation officer would even consider letting me go. Kansas City was one thing, but New York? It wasn't as if I had done a whole lot to earn her trust over the years. I decided to seek out some guidance.

Unsurprisingly, the dean and assistant dean at the ministry

institute were supportive of me pursuing the vision. I figured, *what do I have to lose by asking? It's not like they can revoke my probation for making a request. I'll just see what happens.* As you can tell, I was full of faith when I posed the question.

"Is there any way you'd let me go to New York City for a missions trip?"

"Absolutely, Jed," was her response.

Absolutely, I thought to myself, *really?* Not only did my probation officer approve my travel request; she was excited for me to go.

Now it was real. I didn't know how to plan a missions trip. How was I supposed to raise $1,500 in six weeks? It wasn't as if I could resort to my old ways of making money to fund a missions trip. I sought out my assistant dean, Pastor Ben Fenderson, for direction. He helped me write my inaugural newsletter.

All I wanted to do was try and communicate the vision to people. Using the most sophisticated method I knew, I found this little clipart of a subway train online, stretched it out, and slapped it across the top of the letter. If you can imagine a grainy, disproportionately enlarged picture, you have the idea.

The mission I outlined was pretty simple. We were going to stuff our backpacks with Bibles and hit the NYC subway system and streets, handing Bibles out and sharing our testimonies as we went. Oh, and by the way, we need $1,500. That was the newsletter.

My mailing list consisted of five people. I sent the not-so-professional letter out in faith (at least it had been edited by Ben).

Every penny that was needed came in, plus an additional five hundred. On top of that, we were given three hundred Bibles to take on the trip. There was no turning back now. The travel permit, money, and Bibles had all come in. All that was left was to go.

David, a friend who I met through doing local outreaches, and I boarded the plane bound for LaGuardia Airport in June 2006. My first missions trip. I asked David to accompany me because of his love for and experience with street ministry. He was with me every step of the way throughout two straight weeks of 12-15 hour days spent ministering on the subways and in the streets.

We only had one local church contact in New York, but this individual was able to set us up with a place to stay in Queens Village, Queens. Upon arrival to the home, we discovered that Russian and Indian missionaries who were called to reach the United States were also staying there. It was remarkable to me that people from such distant lands had come to our country to reach the lost.

From our little spot in Queens, we would walk a mile to the bus stop, take a 30-minute ride, and then take a 90-minute train ride into the heart of the city. The sheer volume of people and potential ministry opportunities was overwhelming. Somedays we traveled all the way across the city and only talked to a handful of people. In many of these cases, God highlighted someone for us to talk to and He broke into their life in a powerful way. I remember thinking that it was so worth it even if we only saw one person truly repent and come to Christ.

Jed & David on 1ˢᵗ New York City Mission in 2006

Boldness is something that comes pretty naturally to me, but I was inexperienced in being led by the Spirit. It's one thing to hand someone a tract. It's quite another to follow the Lord's leading when He tells you to speak to or pray for someone. I mostly passed out tracts and Bibles at first, but eventually that helped me move up to ministering to people in a specific way. I had to work through fears, particularly of what people would say to me. Would I have answers to their questions? Could I handle the pressure and criticism? These were New Yorkers, after all, not gentle Minnesotans.

The other battle was my own boundless ambition. There was a drive in me to reach as many people as possible and to keep ministering. Passion is needed to do this type of missions work, but it can be taken to extremes. I would have worked myself and David to the point of exhaustion if I hadn't been kept in check at least a little bit. 12-15 hour days were sufficient. It wasn't as if we were going to reach a city of over eight million in two weeks. The foundation was just being laid on this trip for a more far-reaching work yet to take place.

Towards the end of one of these grueling days of ministry, I was walking alongside a barbwire fence in Queens. Suddenly, I heard a voice say, "Let's Go!" Looking around to see who was talking to me, I realized nobody was there. Then the voice said, "My people are trapped behind the fence. They need to go into the city together with my love."

I sensed that "Let's Go" was a charge to the Church. A charge to the people of God to get ready, prepare your hearts, and go fearlessly in love with the Gospel and share it with everyone. We can't be stuck inside our buildings and comfortable surroundings all the time. There is work to be done.

I believed "Let's Go" to be important, but didn't understand at the time that I had just received my life's mandate. I kept it close to my heart, but didn't tell anyone about it until years later.

This was the literal fence Jed was walking by in Queens

Being in New York City for any length of time really opens your eyes to how diverse America is. Especially for someone like me who had barely traveled and grew up in a predominantly white community. God used this trip to birth in me a heart for the different nations and ethnicities. I left New York with a deep burden for all the people groups on earth to hear the Gospel.

The 1st New Testament Jed handed out in NYC was to a young man named Luis who received prayer and said he knew God had sent them

I returned to the ministry institute with a fresh zeal for outreach. Immediately upon my arrival home, I began planning a second mission. Towards the end of the New York trip, I was on the subway silently asking God where it should be. One of the things on my heart was *cavities*—going to the decayed places in our nation. Riding down the tracks, I heard, "San Francisco". Immediately, I looked up and two girls were sitting across from me dressed in San Francisco gear. That was good enough for me.

Stepping foot into one of the most permissive and godless parts of the United States was quite eye opening. People need Jesus in every city, but the oppression feels even greater in San Francisco. Despite the difficulty of ministering here, we did our best to share the love of Christ on the streets. Although the numbers weren't huge, people were impacted.

I believe that God wanted to continue cultivating a passion for "the one" in my heart, meaning that it's all worth it *just* for one. It means that you would arrange all the details, make the cross country trip, and experience the rejection from many along the way if only it meant impacting one life for eternity. I learned that this mindset was both pleasing to God and necessary so discouragement doesn't overtake you.

Having picked up some valuable on-the-job training, I returned to school. With nine months left at the institute, I had two quarter breaks remaining. I didn't intend to waste them. My winter break would be longer than the others, which gave me time to do a two-week trip. As I had done before, I prayed about the location of my next mission. Once again my heart was drawn to the West Coast.

I had a burden for impacting areas where the hip hop culture was born out of. Drug dealing, promiscuity, money, violence—I wanted to reach into that culture with the light of Christ. It wasn't as if I came from the inner city or that I saw myself as a thug or anything, but I did aspire to live by some of these principles and I had been influenced by this culture. Whether you'd consider me hardcore or a total wannabe doesn't matter. I just wanted to bring the Gospel to some of these places.

My opportunity came on mission trip number three. I decided to pay a visit back to San Francisco for the first week and then made my way south to the Los Angeles area. It was here that I witnessed the ravages of violence and poverty more than any other area I had been to. While ministering on the streets of Compton, I found my car encircled by yellow police tape due to a shooting in broad daylight. Walking up and down the streets of Skid Row in LA revealed to me that thousands of homeless people live in just one single U.S. neighborhood.

It was tempting to be completely overwhelmed by the great need. Not only were so many people trapped in violent, desperate, and seemingly hopeless circumstances, but what exactly did I think I had to offer them? A tract. A bottle of water. A testimony. It all seemed so miniscule compared to the problems they faced. But the Gospel knows no such limitation. Even in these especially dark places, just a simple word, testimony, or prayer touched people deeply. Now it was settled. How could I do anything else with my life but share Jesus?

Back at the center to start my last semester, I began thinking about New York City once again. I had no personal connection to the city or that region, but it was constantly on my heart to return. Rather than questioning why, I started looking ahead to my second missions trip to New York. This would be my final hurrah while under the covering of the ministry institute. I decided to enlist the help of another young believer.

My brother, Hans, had gotten saved and clean from drugs when I was in Teen Challenge. Over the course of a few short months in 2005, my mom was delivered from the burden of worrying about two addicted sons. Her biggest worry then became wondering what might happen to us while ministering in New York City together. Even if this did cause a little stress, I'm sure it was a different feeling for her to be proud of us while worried. The tradeoff was worth it.

In the spring of 2007, David and I flew back to New York to prepare for our second mission there. Hans joined us a few days later. My excitement was overwhelming as I waited for him to land at LaGuardia. The brother who had followed in my dreadful footsteps was going to minister the love of Christ alongside me. Just a year-and-a-half earlier we sat before our mother at Christmas confessing our crimes against her. Now Hans and I were stepping into the mission field together.

We were like an unstoppable tornado of joy. Nobody could shut us up. Former addict brothers on the streets sharing about the undeniable power of God. Some tried to deny it, but there we were in the flesh as living proof of His power! Seeing the light in Hans' eyes again was incredible. I will never forget the look on his face. He had found freedom and was desperate to share the Savior who brought it to him.

It was evident throughout the trip that one of the reasons God kept us alive was so we could minister the Gospel. As Hans and I worked in tandem, there was a love and joy that just flowed out of us. The glory of God was definitely present as we spoke to people. Imagine two exceptionally cheerful and easily excitable young men standing before you passionately relaying the details of their journey from being hopeless drug addicts to followers of Jesus. I'm sure it was a lot for people to take in. But it was real. There was an anointing on the testimony. People saw that restoration with God and family is possible.

There was such a joy in my heart as I returned to Minnesota after my second trip to New York. Ministering with Hans was an amazing experience. This mission was only the first of many opportunities we've had to work together, but I hold this one dearest to my heart. Not only did we get to partner in doing God's work for the first time, but the trip also helped to solidify both of our callings to full-time ministry work.

Hans arrives at LaGuardia Airport for their first joint mission

Time was growing short. Only three months remained before I was to complete the institute and my plans were anything but set. I battled the lies that said my past defined me. Lies that said I couldn't succeed because I'm a felon. Part of me wondered if I could make a living, no matter how meager, doing missions work. But that idea seemed a little out there. I knew that I was called to do some ministry, but couldn't picture how that would work as a full-time job. Making a list of my skills and previous *jobs* confirmed that my only option was going in a brand new direction. How to accomplish that was the perplexing question I had to answer.

Praying through difficulty is one vital thing that I learned from watching the spiritual leaders around me. With no firm direction in mind, I turned to fasting and prayer. Not only was I trying to figure out a job, it was finding housing, and the stress of being on my own soon, where I would have to create structure for myself. Even though I had been clean for over two years at this point, I hadn't been responsible for taking care of all this for myself yet.

I sought counsel from trusted leaders and shared with them my desire to go into full-time ministry. They could see the call of God on my life. One leader after another encouraged me to pursue the vision I sensed the Lord had given. It became settled in my heart. I would become a U.S. based missionary. My network amongst Twin Cities churches was puny, but that didn't matter to me. I finally had a plan, no matter how many holes it seemed to have. Most importantly, I knew the Lord was pleased.

Proudly, I made my way on stage in July of 2007 for the second time in my Teen Challenge career to receive my associate degree in Biblical Studies and Christian Leadership. This time it was five years after my original program graduation and I had completed two full years of ministry training at the institute. It was quite a contrast to my high school graduation where I was high and hungover with a crowd of people looking at me like, how on earth did you pull this off? This time I knew my family, friends, teachers, and mentors were proud of me. Nobody had a concerned look on their face or wondered what kind of trouble I would get myself into now.

I didn't have all the details worked out or know exactly what the next phase of my life would look like. But I knew what I was called to do.

Chapter 10

STEPPING OUT

With an air mattress, two suitcases of belongings, and five monthly supporters, I launched my ministry out of a Northeast Minneapolis house that I shared with two friends. My space was a small side room on the second level. Glamorous it was not. But I was content, and honestly, a little bit scared.

With just $250 coming in every month, there wasn't much room for error. Besides that, people were now entrusting me with their hard-earned money so I could continue to develop the small outreach ministry. Scarier still was the thought that I was accountable to God for being faithful with the money and the work. Sometimes I thought, *Why would God entrust someone like me with all this?* But then I would be reminded that it wasn't about me. God didn't expect polish or perfection.

Rather, He is looking for laborers that will simply step out in obedience and trust Him completely with their lives.

Trusting God was necessary every step of the way. I didn't have a detailed plan for starting the ministry. What I did have was the backing of *Ripe for Harvest World Outreach*, a small missionary sending organization based in Mesa, Arizona. People thought I was a little crazy for going with such a small organization. After all, who wouldn't want the backing of a big ministry or denomination? But for me, a young, ambitious, and fairly clueless missionary, the hands on support they were able to provide was invaluable.

Ripe for Harvest received and distributed contributions on my behalf. This provided me with financial oversight and allowed for donors—mainly friends and family at the time—to receive tax credit for their gifts. I was officially a U.S. based missionary commissioned to do the work of an evangelist. With the endorsement of RFH and a handful of supporters, I was free to begin using my creativity to establish the ministry.

Not knowing exactly how to go about developing the work, I decided to start with the basics. I established an early morning routine of prayer and worship right away. In some ways I was used to doing this from being in the program, but the main difference now was that nobody was forcing me to spend time seeking God. After three straight years of mandated chapels and prayer, I had to start holding myself accountable.

The other area I decided to focus on was setting a schedule. My last experience with scheduling was figuring out the most advantageous times of day to sell drugs. Now I had to learn what a missionary's week should look like. Although it wouldn't be a straight 9-5 job due to the nature of the work, I chose to approach it as regular full-time job. If this was to be my occupation, I needed to work at least as hard at it as I would a traditional job. It's a miracle in and of itself that someone like me could set, maintain, and be accountable to a self-regulated schedule, but somehow I found the grace to do it.

Living with my two roommates also helped during this initial launch phase. They too had ministry callings on their lives and the three of us would spend time sharing our ideas. Discussing the things we were feeling lead by the Lord to do in the short- and long-term spurred all of us on. It definitely encouraged me to be faithful with the daily outreach work I was trying to establish.

These were truly days of small beginnings. Here I was a four-time felon with no name recognition and little formal education trying to start a brand new ministry. Despite my pioneering spirit, it was a bit intimidating to stare down those facts. Thankfully, the Holy Spirit was continuously in my ear nudging me on, "Jed, I have people for you to reach. Trust me. I will lead the way. I will provide for you."

My heart would swell with encouragement as I sensed these words from God. I was constantly being reminded that seeming hindrances in the natural are not obstacles to God's will. His wisdom somehow causes hindrances to work to your advantage. This fact became clear during the earliest days.

Buses quickly became one of my most effective ministry tools. I didn't own a vehicle, nor would I have been able to afford driving one, so on a near daily basis I took the bus into downtown Minneapolis. People in all sorts of different life circumstances ride the bus. Some are traveling to a job where they make a comfortable living, others are destitute. Many are addicts, dropouts, or both. Still others are just ordinary people schlepping their way through life. It didn't matter to the Lord what their circumstances were. He loved them all deeply and poured that into me so I could share it.

I would step onto that bus bursting with the love of God. The fire of the Gospel burned in my heart as I brought His message of hope and truth to people. Sometimes I would simply ask individuals if they needed prayer. Usually there was a willingness to receive this type of ministry and it opened the door for people to hear that they desperately needed a Savior. I kneeled on the bus floor with many, clasping hands with them as they asked Jesus for salvation.

It was amazing to see the momentum build as the Lord would impact one person. Pretty soon someone else on the bus who had witnessed the encounter would ask me to pray for them. Sometimes this would just keep going on as the Holy Spirit spread like wildfire. Now I don't want to give the impression that I was like Charles Finney, seeing miracles and revival break out every time I took public transportation. There were times when it was dry and I dealt with many rejections along the way. Regardless, there was never a lack of opportunity. I would think to myself, *Wow, the bus is a great mission field; who needs a car?*

These early experiences opened my eyes to a lifestyle of mission. Formal outreaches, crusades, and events are all great ways to reach people, but they aren't the only ones. The Lord used the ministry's initial season of development where things were very organic and informal to teach me a foundational principle: outreach is continual. This doesn't mean that you have to reach out to every single person you encounter for the rest of your life. It's more of a paradigm shift from thinking that evangelism is an event to understanding that evangelism is a way of life. This mindset shaped the development of the ministry.

Aside from the bus ministry as I made my way around the city, spontaneous witnessing was a staple of the early work. I'd take my backpack full of tracts and New Testaments to hand out on the Minneapolis streets. Sometimes alone and other times with friends accompanying, I'd share my testimony, pray, and preach along the way. We didn't discriminate against any type of person. No matter who it was, if the Lord lead us to reach out to an individual, we did our best to obey. God didn't discriminate either. Every day we witnessed Him impact lives through salvation, healing, and deliverance. Sometimes it was a junkie; other times it was a business professional.

One time outside of a steakhouse, I encountered a doctor who had a heart condition. "God knows how to heal you," I said to him.

Wide-eyed, he replied, "I didn't tell you I was sick."

"God knows your greatest need."

This gentleman allowed me to pray for him and expressed that he felt a shift in his heart. I don't know exactly what happened in his body that evening since I never saw him again, but I do know the Holy Spirit revealed to me that he was ill. These types of impressions, sometimes faint and sometimes clear as a bell, opened doors to be able to pray with so many people. They were always amazed that God cared enough to reveal such a personal word about them.

Another time there was a group of young men walking toward me on the street. One of them in particular was highlighted to me. Suddenly, I had a vision of a knife and this kid. I greeted him when he walked past, but he glared at me and kept walking. I yelled after him, "You don't want to give up today. God is waiting for you to place your hurt in His hands."

He whipped around with his friends listening and said to me, "I cut myself to drive away the pain."

As I looked into his eyes with compassion, I watched as the Holy Spirit violently tore this kid's walls down. He listened intently as I shared the Good News of a God who loved him enough to die for him. Then he pulled out the knife he used to mutilate his body in a desperate attempt to escape his pain. He handed it over to me and prayed to receive eternal life.

These kinds of encounters are incredible to experience. Some people struggle with believing in a personal God who cares about the affairs of man. But little doubt can remain after you witness a life transformed before your eyes and no reasonable explanation exists other than God. He cares enough to reveal specific details about a person or situation and then makes sure those details are presented in such a way that they will be understood.

I think of Jesus speaking to the Samaritan woman at the well in the fourth chapter of the Gospel of John. He spoke to her with extreme clarity about her life situation. It was direct and specific. She was so impacted by meeting Jesus that she went into her village and told everyone about Him. The Bible tells us that many came to believe in Jesus because of her witness. He truly desires to minister personally to individuals, and when He does, the impact is astounding. This woman, who would have been considered a whore by many people, ended up pointing her community to Jesus. He can take the most unlikely person and make them His witness.

This is exactly how I felt many days. It was still a bit surreal to be living as a missionary. I wasn't sure if I was doing it right. I mean, shouldn't the ministry grow faster, be more effective, reach bigger crowds? I started to feel a little stuck and perhaps a bit impatient. Writing the monthly newsletter to my small base of supporters was challenging. Sure, there were some cool testimonies from the buses and streets, but was it enough? I was grinding out the regular outreach work, taking a few speaking opportunities, and doing short-term missions trips, but the scope of the work was still very small. And there was another longing in my heart that I couldn't seem to shake.

It was 2008 and I was in the midst of trying to plow a trail for the ministry. This was hard work with opposition around every corner. It was also lonely at times. Though I desired marriage someday, I was not expecting to find myself deeply entwined in a relationship as quickly as it happened. But there I was. Before I could even catch my breath, I was swept up in a sea of emotion and desire.

The relationship was fraught with problems from the start. It's funny how clear a situation can be to your friends when you are completely blind to the reality. Suddenly boundaries went out the window. We quickly found ourselves alone together on multiple occasions. The kissing with heavy touching was justified in our minds as innocent enough since we were planning to get married. Then one day it went way too far.

My friends had tried to warn me. In fact, I have friends who would tell you today just how horrified they were by the relationship. They knew the call of God on my life and were terribly grieved by the thought of me throwing it away. Despite the pleadings of these friends, I found myself in sexual sin. The writing had been on the wall; it was only a matter of time.

Spiraling into a deep depression, I thought my life as a missionary was over. My sin weighed heavily upon me. Miraculously, I didn't turn to drugs or alcohol, but I felt hopeless. Here the Lord had delivered me from so much and given me this precious ministry to steward. How could I possibly screw it up so badly? I figured there was no way He would trust me with it again.

After confessing my sin to a spiritual father of mine, Pastor Jeff Dye, I entered into a time of restoration. He wisely instructed me that I needed to step back from the relationship altogether so God could deal with me and bring healing. If God really wanted this relationship to happen, it would be worth setting aside for a season so it could develop in His time.

Tears streamed down my face as Pastor Jeff prayed and spoke words of encouragement over me. "This season is not the end, Jed, this will not ruin you. It will help you grow into a greater man of God."

The presence of the Lord was so strong in his office throughout the meeting. Yes, God was reaffirming the call on my life, but more importantly, He was reaffirming my calling as His son. The fellowship between us had been interrupted by this sin, but He wanted me back! It wasn't just about being busy doing ministry; it was about my heart—my whole heart—being surrendered to Him in a loving relationship. More temptations would come, but staying in deep communion with Him would give me the power to overcome them.

But if we confess our sins to him, he is faithful and just to forgive us our sins and to cleanse us from all wickedness. 1 John 1:9

Throughout the weeks and months that followed, friends came alongside to help me through. I went from feeling completely alone and hopeless to experiencing a level of love and comfort I had never felt. Joy followed repentance. From that time forward, I really began walking with the Holy Spirit on a daily basis. I had definitely encountered Him before on many occasions, but now it became a deeper fellowship. I became much more sensitive to His leading after going through this season of sin, brokenness, and restoration.

Chapter 11

MISTAKES REDEEMED

*Let all that I am praise the LORD; may I never forget
the good things he does for me. He forgives all my sins
and heals all my diseases. He redeems me from death
and crowns me with love and tender mercies.* Psalm 103:2-4

Six months after beginning my restoration process, I
received a rather ironic speaking invitation. A pastor in
Wisconsin wanted me to share at his youth camp about purity.
After much prayer, I felt released by the Holy Spirit to accept
the invitation.

At this point in my four-year-long Christian journey, I had
publicly shared about my struggles with drug and alcohol
addiction many times. My issues with sexual sin were another
story, but I chose to open up to these teenagers. I discussed my

battle with pornography, sexual sin, and my recent moral failure. This experience affected me deeply. While I trust my testimony was helpful for the youth to hear, going public with my struggle brought me to new levels of freedom. So much shame and guilt surround this arena that it is very difficult to break through. But there is grace to walk in purity. Grace to live in freedom from shame.

Emerging from this period of restoration was a kind of new birth for me. Before my descent into sexual sin, I had been sincere and passionate about my faith. Afterwards, a new level of intensity came over me. Only this time my zeal was coupled with far greater maturity. There is nothing quite as humbling as knowing that you are capable of throwing everything away in the blink of an eye. In just a matter of weeks, I had gone from being a sold-out missionary to hiding in shame, having disgraced God and the ministry. I no longer lived in that shame after this time of repentance, but I walked in the humility that comes from understanding one's brokenness.

I decided it was time to start traveling again and fully engage back in the work. My friend Steven and I started planning a trip to New York City that would have us going to some very challenging places. Our key targets were to be The Bowery, Williamsburg Hasidic Jewish Community, and Wall Street. We would cover a diverse cross section of the poor, religious, and wealthy by hitting these locations.

As soon as we touched down, we started traveling about the city, praying and seeking God for direction. Suddenly, as we were traversing the streets and subway system, I was reminded of an outreach idea that had been lying dormant in my heart for many months. I stopped to tell Steven the vision I had for

Subway Church.

"That sounds awesome—we need to do this," Steven said.

"Alright, we'll try it tomorrow."

The reality of what this might look like smacked me in the face. Up until this point, I had primarily done one-on-one ministry. I didn't preach to crowds on the streets. I didn't walk into public places and pronounce a message. Yet here I was, contemplating openly speaking to an entire New York City Subway. I could think of many times in the past where I apprehensively clutched my Bible on the train. A message would be burning on my heart to share with everyone, but the words wouldn't come out. Fear got the best of me.

We got on at the Wall Street Station. *Am I really going to do it this time?* I asked myself. Then it came. Like a sudden shift of the wind, a boldness came upon me and Steven. Before my humanity or reason could catch up with me, I announced, "Hey, everyone! I just want to thank you for coming to Subway Church. I believe God has something supernatural and special for you today...we will not be taking up an offering and everything we have to offer to you today is free."

Our approach during Subway Church was personal and respectful. We didn't shout at people with a message about damnation and judgment. Rather, we shared our own testimonies of finding freedom in Christ and weaved the Gospel in through our real life stories. No matter what approach you take, there are some people that simply won't respond to being told they need a savior or that they are doing wrong and will have to answer to God for it. The message is difficult to present regardless of method, but there is a way to bring it that doesn't automatically cause people to put their guard up.

My first experience with Subway Church was unbelievable. To have an idea like this on your heart and actually follow through with it is very exhilarating. We found this method of ministry has some interesting nuances. You have basically a captive audience for at least brief stretches of time in between stops. Then the doors open, some people exit and new ones come on. Each time we would welcome people to Subway Church and then continue sharing our testimonies and the Gospel. It was brand new to Steven and I, so we didn't have all the best practices and details worked out. But we know God honored our obedience and the sharing of His Word.

One young woman continued to make her way towards us car to car from the opposite end of the train. She sat down close enough to make out what we were saying. As she listened intently to the message, God was moving on her heart in a powerful way. After getting our attention to come speak with her, she told us that we seemed to be genuine and that she thought we actually cared about the people we were speaking to. This young woman from East Harlem surrendered her life to the Lord right there on the train. She would be the first, but thankfully not the last person to do so.

Subway Church became a staple of our New York City and other metro area missions. It is such a powerful opportunity to reach people. Some on the trains no doubt think this is an incredible interruption to their day. But others understand that out of all the trains in the city we could have been on, we were on theirs and God was trying to speak to them. Over time, worship teams were added whenever possible to sing and play music onboard. We also began to incorporate one-on-one ministry rather than only speaking to the crowds. I have seen women trapped in prostitution surrender their lives to Jesus and wealthy men cry as we pray with them to be reconciled to their children. God moves on these mass transit systems.

Ever since that first awkward step of obedience into launching Subway Church, both me and Steven have walked in much greater boldness. There is something about obedience that unlocks deeper levels in the things of God. Openness about one's weaknesses also brings you to deeper levels. After sharing about my struggles with purity at the youth camp and then trusting God to help me preach openly on the subway, I felt like I had come into far greater freedom. This was true, but there were still a few things I was holding onto. I didn't anticipate what the Lord had planned for me to learn and experience on my next mission.

Jed & Steven's first Subway Church

As I searched for what avenue God might lead me down next, an unexpected opportunity came up. A ministry to bikers that was venturing into Sturgis, South Dakota for the world famous Sturgis® Motorcycle Rally™, invited me to serve alongside them. I never was a biker and hadn't specifically ministered to this group of people before. However, it certainly was an interesting open door and a good opportunity to continue growing in boldness. There are, perhaps, few groups of people more intimidating to minister to than bikers. Little did I know that this seemingly random missions trip would open my eyes to a vital truth that I hadn't previously understood.

The outreach was setup so the workers had time to encounter God personally through worship and prayer before going out to minister. This way wasn't about trying to muster up your courage to go talk to someone like I had done so many times before. It was about experiencing the heart of God in a real way and then being sent out in that love to deliver the transforming message of the Gospel to people. Confidence comes from the Holy Spirit when you are in a place of fellowship with Him; not from your own strength or boldness.

Yes, I am the vine; you are the branches. Those who remain in me, and I in them, will produce much fruit. For apart from me you can do nothing. John 15:5

Experiencing worship, prayer, and outreach together was revolutionary. It drove me once again into deeper places with God and forced me out of do-it-yourself ministry. Slipping into a mode of working for God with little requested assistance from Him is quite easy. That's not to say that He abandons us in our ministry if we're not praying enough. All good fruit from anything we do is because of Him. But our nature is to attempt self-reliance rather than be desperate for God's help. This doesn't automatically change just because you're doing missions work. I hadn't realized that in all my working *for* God, I had lost some of that vital connection *to* God.

As the outreach progressed, they had a time of personal ministry for the workers. I walked up to a man for prayer. Clutching my hands, he said, "Brother, what you have done has been erased in the precious blood of Jesus—move on and let God have everything."

I sat down to feverishly scribble out my thoughts on a scrap of paper. My struggles, reservations, fears—things I had been clinging to for way too long. I crumbled up the paper, tossed it in the garbage, and thought, *It's time to run with God, no regrets.*

Chapter 12

BROUGHT TOGETHER

I sat in prayer on the Long Beach sand of New York City in May of 2009. Suddenly, I felt the Lord say, "Ask Me anything in My Name and I will give it to you."

This is the time to have your list of needs ready to go, but I couldn't think of anything. Then the yearning for a wife emerged above any other request I could muster. At this point, I had been setting aside my desire for a relationship for many months. Perhaps this was an indication from God that He was about to move in this area of my life.

Erica grew up in northern Minnesota, where a godly couple had practically adopted and loved her as their own daughter. The Sayler family was very active in their local church. Their small congregation, located 150 miles north of the Twin Cities in Duluth, had been the very first church to contribute to my missions trips in 2006. True to form, Stan and Angela Sayler were eager to support a young missionary. They kept in touch after our initial meeting and offered a place for me to stay whenever I came up north to minister. Meanwhile, Erica was roughing it in Florida as a children's pastor at a small church.

Over time, I got to know the Saylers quite well—apparently well enough for them to trust me with a beloved member of their family. As any good Christian parent with a single daughter approaching thirty might do, Stan and Angela began encouraging Erica to get in touch with me, their also-approaching-thirty, single missionary friend. We chatted on Facebook a few times, but in all honesty, I didn't really see a romantic relationship coming. In all fairness, that's probably due to my denseness; Erica saw the potential from the beginning.

"Jed, is there any way you could pick me up from the Minneapolis airport and drive me to Duluth?" Erica asked.

Although I had just returned from the New York trip where God had spoken to me on the beach, the connection between that encounter and Erica's request was somehow lost on me.

"Sure, I just returned from New York, but I could use a few days to unwind and see my friends."

I had no idea that this woman I was meeting for the first time in May of 2009 would become my wife the following summer. We chatted as we made our way up I-35 to the newly thawed out tundra of what is affectionately referred to as the "Northland". There was a comfortability right away between the two of us, but it would take me a while to realize how, and with whom, God was answering my prayers.

Our Facebook chats continued here and there, but when Erica moved back to Minnesota in December, we began spending time together. About a month after she came back, I went to Duluth for a ski weekend. I'm embarrassed to admit that I was actually interested in another girl at the time and even asked Erica for advice in pursuing that relationship. Man, was I ever thick, but I'm not sure she is much better. Erica has since confessed that she was praying for God to put an end to whatever was going on with *the other girl*. Thankfully, it didn't take long for me to realize she wasn't interested in me anyways.

After two weeks of being in near constant contact with Erica—either in person or via text and Facebook—it became clear that the other relationship I was pursuing wasn't going anywhere. It was Super Bowl Sunday when that dream officially died. You might be tempted to think that I was a real jerk. I mean, how could I be pursuing this other woman when Erica was standing right in front of me? But I really was blind to what now seems so obvious.

A few days after, Erica and I were chatting on Facebook and I mentioned how hungry I was.

"I'd bring you some dinner if you didn't live so far away, she responded."

"Maybe I could take you out for Valentine's Day and we could have dinner then…as friends, of course."

Erica agreed to my Valentine's dinner as *friends* plan, but this quickly evolved into our first date on February 14, 2010.

There was almost an immediate understanding between the two of us that we were to be together. Erica and I started discussing our future very seriously right away. Just three weeks later, on March 7th, I proposed at beautiful Split Rock Lighthouse on the shore of Lake Superior.

Erica was thinking ahead to the following February as a good time for the wedding, but I'm not the type to exhibit that kind of patience. We were married on August 21, 2010 at a small church in Duluth, just six months after we started dating.

I had spent three years trying to plot and plan my way into marriage, but when the Lord moved in His timing and brought Erica to me, it all just happened organically. I did my best to mess things up in this area of my life, but God's mercy and grace overcame all my failures. He knew that I needed a partner who would be fully aligned with His will for our lives as a couple. At this point, we had barely even begun to realize some of the things He was calling us to do.

God didn't give us much time to catch our breath before throwing us in the deep end together.

Chapter 13

LET'S GO

"I'm pregnant." Erica and I had been married for three months when she broke the news that we were already expecting our first child together. I was thrilled at the thought of a baby, but it was very soon. We were still living with friends in Duluth at the time and hadn't planned on our family being jumpstarted so quickly.

While on our honeymoon three months earlier, we had decided to move to Florida after agreeing in prayer about what our next move should be. We had a sense that God was saying to us, "Grow roots and branch out." We just didn't realize at the time that it would mean moving and getting settled with Erica pregnant. Not to mention relocating myself as a missionary in a city that was brand new to me. I wasn't sure what direction the ministry would take after the move.

On December 27, 2010, Erica and I said our last goodbyes to family and set out on the 1,500-mile drive to Daytona Beach. It was sorrowful leaving behind so many loved ones in Minnesota, but we strongly felt God's hand on the decision. We were off to establish our family and impact new communities for Christ.

After three-and-a-half years of serving as a missionary under Ripe for Harvest World Outreach, we decided it was time to launch the ministry that had been stirring in me since 2006. *Lets Go Ministry, Inc.* would become an official nonprofit in February of 2011. Named for the cry God had put in my heart years earlier, LGM's formation would bring about the expansion and refinement of the work that began years earlier with a single trip to New York City.

With His guiding hand, Lets Go Ministry has grown into a Kingdom fire on earth. We share His love with everyone we possibly can. At the writing of this book, we've ministered in twenty-six states and five countries. I have visited New York City more than twenty times over the past decade.

I spent the first four years of my ministry primarily doing local outreach and speaking, as well as traveling back and forth to New York and a handful of other cities. I shared about God in the streets and subways, in the sun and rain, in the spring and fall in the U.S., but while in New York during one trip, God birthed in me a heart for the nations. At first, I didn't really know what to make of this call to international ministry. I saw myself as a domestic missionary. There was more than enough work to do in my own state and nation; how could I even think about ministering abroad? Besides, I couldn't leave the country even if I wanted to.

Shortly after our move to Florida, I was assigned to a Christian probation officer. He believed the change in my life was genuine and decided it was time for me to be released. When the judge allowed me to go back to Minnesota Adult & Teen Challenge in 2004, he sentenced me to twenty years of probation. It was understandable for a repeat offender like me. But my new PO had seen enough and put me up for early completion in 2012—nine years before my scheduled date. The main hindrance to international ministry had been cleared away practically overnight.

Not long after my release from probation, I received an invitation from a friend of a friend to visit Colombia. He had done missions work over the years in and around the city of Barranquilla on the northern coast. His hope was to inspire a young missionary by showing how desperately the region needed ongoing work and how ripe the area was for ministry. This veteran missionary was getting older and was hoping someone else would catch the vision.

Peace flooded my soul as I descended into Barranquilla for the first time in July of 2012. During the flight, I had an open vision. There was a large field being worked by many farmers. They were harvesting their crops and helping the poor. As I entered the field, I saw with my eyes a people who knew hardship and persecution. I was entering into a field where the laborers had prepared a ripe harvest field. In the vision, I shook hands with the farmers and then began working with them.

I came out of the vision as we were descending onto the runway. Suddenly, I smelled smoke from a nearby fire and saw an airport that looked like it was from the 70s. Joy flooded my heart as I landed on the promise of God that my feet would see foreign soil. I had carried the Gospel to another place and was ready to pour out.

The first message I preached in Colombia was from Proverbs 25:25, "Good news from far away is like cold water to the thirsty."

Afterwards, I saw a woman walking with a cane. I asked, "Can I pray for you to be healed and strengthened?"

"Sure, I was just on my way to the hospital to see a doctor."

I prayed over her and she was healed on the spot.

"Well, I'll still go to the doctor and tell him what happened to me."

"Jesus healed you, not me." She smiled as she walked away.

See, that is cold and refreshing water to a thirsty soul! Jesus still heals today and He does it supernaturally through His church; His people. So when we humble ourselves, He uses us.

I saw this same woman at church two days later and she had brought friends with her. She surrendered her life to Jesus that morning at the altar. I thought to myself, *no one can make this stuff up. It's all Jesus!*

Being in Barranquilla gave me a heart for ministering to the masses. At one point in my life, I thought mass evangelism was only for those guys on TV with the nice suits and white hair. I figured most of it was fake and that many were in it for the money. But then I saw the power of it with my own two eyes. I witnessed salvation, healing, and deliverance happen on a much deeper level than I was used to seeing. All I could think was that I wanted to see Jesus move in power more and more. I cannot attest to the purity or value of all mass evangelism that is being done today, but I believe now that it has an important role to play in reaching communities, and even whole regions and nations with the Gospel.

During my first mission, we visited many schools, prisons, and hospitals. We also ministered to families in the streets and went door-to-door throughout the city. I met the principal of a local school at church and he invited me to speak to the kids. We saw over 300 precious youth surrender their hearts to Jesus that day. It didn't stop there. After the service, the principal wanted our team to pray for everyone who wanted prayer.

I figured no one at a Middle School/Junior High would come to this little classroom for prayer, but for the next four hours, the classroom filled up, emptied, then filled up again. There was a line out the door. The common theme was that the kids felt neglected, set aside, and unsafe. Some knew Jesus already and wanted us to lay our hands on them and pray over their life. The Holy Spirit moved in power over these young ones. This was the day I received a heart for the masses.

Not long after my initial trip to Colombia, God started laying a burden on my heart that He wanted to raise "minor leaguers" up to do "major league" ministry. We have a minor league baseball stadium in Daytona Beach and I started thinking about the possibility of doing a mass evangelism event at the stadium one day. I also began to immediately consider going back to Colombia and making preparations to do an event there.

From 2012 to 2014, we went through the planning stages for our first ever Gospel campaign in a stadium. It was a small one, but it was a stadium and I was stoked! It was to be held at the Velodromo of Barranquilla, a small bicyclist stadium. I had never done anything like it before, but it seemed the more I stepped out with what I knew God wanted me to do—usually in small things—the more He unlocked doors to the bigger things.

I made several trips during the planning phase to build relationships with the local churches in Barranquilla and help mobilize people. There was no way my small team of a couple people from the U.S. was going to pull it off alone. And even if we could pull it off alone, we believed strongly in working closely with the local churches so those who came to the event could get connected and discipled.

Working alongside these faithful believers was amazing. Sure, there were some cultural differences and other challenges we encountered, but the Colombian churches were capable of putting outreaches together with little time and resource. This allowed us to spend significant amounts of our time ministering in the streets, door-to-door, and other places during these prep trips. There is a lot of desperation in Colombia and we had some unbelievable opportunities to minister to people. One such experience I will never forget.

After a long morning of ministering, I headed back to the place we were staying to rest. Before I could lie down, a young boy came to the door with a local pastor whom I was working with. Pastor Romo explained that this young boy had a message for the missionaries. His grandmother witnessed her son's murder—just fifteen feet away from her—a few days before. She wanted us to come pray with her.

I left with the boy and Pastor Romo. While we walked, the atmosphere just felt supernaturally charged. We arrived to find the entire family crammed into a small house with no air conditioning. Everyone was sweating from head to toe. The mother sat in her chair, weeping. The family stood in silence.

There isn't a whole lot you can say to make a situation like this easier. Only God can bring hope to such devastated people. I asked the Holy Spirit to comfort the family. We sat with them for an hour as the presence of God permeated the tiny space. More people arrived. Soon we couldn't move. We prayed again. The Lord began encountering individuals in a powerful way. Every single person in the house surrendered their life to Jesus. To this day, the family, including the young boy's grandmother, actively serves in the local church right in the same community where she witnessed the awful tragedy.

Unfortunately, not all of our encounters during the two years of preparation felt so glorious. While planning for the *Freedom Experience*, we encountered a raging battle. We went through serious financial difficulties. I personally faced and battled against depression and frustration. When I arrived in Colombia for the final two weeks of preparation before the event, I found out the City of Barranquilla did not approve our application to rent the stadium. But I had come too far.

I went to my friend and event coordinator for help. Going in faith, we marched into the office at the stadium. We didn't know who to talk to or what we were doing, so we just kept going. The Holy Spirit must have opened many locked doors or something along the way, because we ended up being able to walk right into the stadium and stood at the person's door who could help us. We told him about our issues with renting the stadium and he said to give him a few days to work on it. We waited and waited. Finally, I received a call saying that not only had we been approved to rent, but they wanted to let us use the stadium for free.

I'm not sure how it all happened, but many churches were mobilized into action, trained up, and sent out all over the city for the final week of ministry leading up to the Freedom Experience. But it was a mess. Money went missing and we were quickly running out of it. When the doors opened for the first night of the event, one young kid sat in the stands. That was it. I quickly gathered the intercessors to pray. They assured me the people would come once the sun went down. Not being as faith-filled as the intercessors, I sat in the stands and cried with the kid.

Then it happened. Just like the locals had promised me, people started showing up once it grew dark. A worship team appeared seemingly out of nowhere and began to play. Pastors and other leaders filed in. We were ready to start...two hours after I had planned.

Second night came. Same thing. Only this time I did something besides crying. As I was praying in the back room, the Holy Spirit told me to go outside and walk around the stadium. So I did. As I was walking around with my assistant, some intercessors, and others, the love of God began to rise up inside of me. I began to shout with joy and tears, "Come inside and experience the freedom only God can give! Come on, come on everyone. This will be an evening you will never forget!"

I thought to myself, *If this thing is going to fail, I am going to give it all I got!* Then I went inside and the buses we had sent to the highly impoverished communities began to arrive with many poor people from all over the city. There were many sick and diseased as well, expecting God to move in a mighty way. The fire of God was so amazing during worship that I found myself looking around thinking, *Nothing will stop the move of God here tonight!*

On the main level, there were hundreds of people, and in the stands, there were a couple hundred more. There, in the stands, I saw a man we had ministered to in the streets during our pre-event outreaches. He surrendered his life to Jesus and we had lunch with him. He brought his brother to the Freedom Experience, and at the end of the night, he and his brother came forward to the packed altar to give their hearts to God together! It was one of the most beautiful things I have ever seen. I looked at my friend, Colin, who had labored with me in that mission and we smiled from ear to ear.

There were reports from the churches of many new souls added to their congregations. We have since met many of them. Others were physically healed. An 83-year-old crippled woman was healed and walked onto the bus at the end of the night. Families were restored during the two nights—a fulfillment of the vision we had for the event all along. The church was mobilized, engaged, and in love with Jesus. We still work with many of these precious friends today in Colombia.

Jed and the first little boy that was in the stands

It became clear over my first five trips to Colombia that God was calling Lets Go Ministry to ongoing work in the country. What shape this will take over the years remains to be seen. All I know for sure at the writing of this book is that the Lord has amazing things in store for the nation of Colombia. We hope to be a small part of His work there.

Chapter 14

RESTORATION

I walked to the mailbox one day after returning home from an exhausting trip to Barranquilla. An envelope with the return address of the department of family and protective services sat on top. Nervously, I hurried into the house to open it in front of Erica. My heart raced as I began to read the letter.

Erica touched my arm. "What is it, Jed?"

"It's about Rosella. I believe she is my daughter. They want to get in touch with me about something that has happened to her."

It had never been confirmed before that Rosella—a girl that I fathered during a six-month on-again, off-again relationship—was in fact my daughter. Erica knew when we got married that I might have a daughter. I never tried to keep it from her.

When Rosella was born, my name wasn't included on her birth certificate. I stayed with her birth mom for a few months, but I was in the throes of my addiction and in no position to be an effective parent. I soon left Rosella's mother and we agreed it was best to keep her in the care of her grandparents. I always questioned if I did the right thing.

I read the letter with memories of this little girl flitting through my mind. The Holy Spirit saturated me with grace and peace. I knew my past failures would not dictate my future and God would turn it around for good. More importantly, this young girl needed my help. Who knows what happened to her or what she was going through? Right now she needed a dad to step up and care for her. I knew immediately that I was to take responsibility and seek out if Rosella was really my daughter.

After reading the letter, Erica and I called the number enclosed. "Is she okay?" Erica asked, showing compassion for a person she didn't know. She wanted to know why I didn't try harder to find this girl. I asked myself that same question countless times, but I lost touch with the grandparents and mother. I had convinced myself that not knowing meant Rosella must be in a safe place. She wasn't.

I spoke with the case worker. She informed us that Rosella had been placed in foster care after being abused. Learning the truth about what she had endured was like being stabbed in the chest. Through tears, I looked at Erica. Tears rolled down her cheeks. When I hung up and without saying a word, I knew Erica and I would care for Rosella. The case worker asked me to take a paternity test through a court order. Erica and I agreed that even if I wasn't the biological father, God would have us care for this young girl. In my heart, though, I already knew the result—Rosella was my daughter and we'd go to any lengths to get her.

For the next few days, I couldn't stop thinking about Rosella. The story of her abuse and the reality of what she may be feeling sunk deep into my spirit. I couldn't shake it off. To think that I could have prevented what happened to her was almost an unbearable pill to swallow. But there was no way for me to undo the damage. All I could do was pray that God would allow me to be part of the healing process and have a second chance to be a father to her. I grew increasingly impatient every day thinking of Rosella sitting in foster care as we waited for God to bring her to us.

Erica and I cried and prayed together over the situation. We both had a strong sense of confirmation that Rosella would be joining our family one day. I knew my Heavenly Father would have to work this situation out with my background. Court systems don't typically place an abused child under the custody of a convicted felon, but we strongly believed God's hand was on it. Yet, I couldn't help but wonder how He would work it out.

After years of ministering to boys and girls and seeing the miracles God had done for them, was He working one in the life of my daughter? Yes, I had left behind a little girl when I should have done more and I didn't *deserve* a second chance. But with God, it's not about deserving anything. He knew this was the time to bring me and Rosella back together. At no other time in my life could I have taken her in. I couldn't have cared for her up until then. He knew that and now was giving me a second chance with the daughter I never thought I'd see again.

Erica said that God had placed it on her heart weeks before

the letter came that she would care for a young girl, someone who was in need of help. In my heart, this felt like a mission from heaven. Rosella became our greatest mission to date. The DNA test confirmed she was my biological daughter. What joy, what relief, what pain from years past—wasted years that God would now begin to restore.

As I collected my luggage at the Miami International Airport after a mission to Colombia, my mind and heart brimmed with anticipation. The next day, July 28, 2014, was the day I was to be reunited with Rosella. It would be the first time we had laid eyes on each other since she was a baby. Rosella kept a photo of me in case she ever did meet her daddy, but that was all she knew of me.

I landed in Dallas and drove the hundred miles as fast as I reasonably could to the courthouse. And there she was. Now a beautiful teenager instead of the cute baby girl I remembered, Rosella embraced me and I could not hold back the tears from streaming down my face. After all those years of distance, I still sensed an immediate connection to her.

Rosella and I enjoyed almost an instant familiarity. The case worker allowed me to take her to lunch before the hearing and we talked as if we had known one another all along. What a tremendous blessing it was to be together and start building our relationship right away. She wasn't full of anger and resentment towards me; I wouldn't have blamed her if she was. However, this was only the beginning. We had a long ways to go in building the kind of loving, trusting bond that can only come with time. But we were finally reunited and starting a journey that would contain many twists and turns in the future.

During the hearing, I spoke with the judge and he granted me a two week visit, so Rosella left with me that very day! She cried tears of joy in knowing she would get to meet her dad and his family, but also tears of sorrow in leaving her siblings behind in Texas. Two brothers and three sisters would remain in foster care while Rosella traveled with me to Florida.

We stayed on for a few days in Texas and celebrated my thirty-fourth birthday together at the top of the Reunion Tower in downtown Dallas. Later that night, we enjoyed a baseball game. Over our first couple of days together, we ate steaks, ribs, and all the best food Texas had to offer. We enjoyed every minute of being with one another. It was a dream come true.

The night before we flew to Florida, Rosella told me something I will never forget. "Dad, I have a picture of you holding me when I was a baby. I always wanted to know who my real dad was. God answered my prayer!"

I was in tears. The regret of the wasted years was thick. There was such joy in our reunion, but I couldn't help but think what could have been if I hadn't resigned myself to the life of a junkie. Rosella's mom said it was either me or one other guy who was her father. I should have pursued the truth back then. But I didn't. I'm not sure if I figured she was better off without a father like me or if I was just too selfish and immature to face up to my responsibility. Probably some of both. Regardless, it was time to move forward.

When we landed in Florida to finish out the remaining ten days of our visit, I did not anticipate what would happen next. I placed a call to the judge to try and lobby for an extended visit. Not only was the extension granted, Rosella ended up staying with us permanently! In April of 2015, I was awarded full custody of Rosella.

A couple of years prior to my reunification with Rosella, God highlighted an outreach to me that would focus on bringing families together—the *Freedom Experience*. These 2-night events at small stadiums would allow families to come together for activities, music, and to hear the Gospel. After a couple of years of thinking about it, the LGM Board decided it was time to pursue this in 2014. This project was in the works for so long that I couldn't possibly have imagined that my daughter would be restored to me the week of the Colombia event and just a couple of months prior to the Florida one. The mission of the Freedom Experience was to see households saved, the hearts of the fathers turned to their children, and the fatherless brought back into relationship with their family. This very reality unfolded in my life as fruit of the Holy Spirit at work.

Father to the fatherless, defender of widows—this is God, whose dwelling is holy. God places the lonely in families; he sets the prisoners free and gives them joy... Psalm 68:5-6

Jed and Rosella at the Freedom Experience in Daytona Beach

Adjusting to our expanded family had unique challenges for all of us. Annabelle was two-and-a-half and Lydia was just one. Now they had a teenage sister living with them and Rosella had two very little siblings. All of us were brand new to Rosella and she had left behind the family and state that she knew to be with us. Erica and I had to figure out how to best tend to the needs of our young ones and a teenager, which was a totally new experience for us. Needless to say, it was a wild time in the Lindstrom household. But God had prepared us in advance for these challenges.

Throughout the years of doing ministry, Erica and I had learned how to walk in love and grace alongside people who were struggling. Both of us know what it is like to be the one in need and to serve those in need. We definitely have made mistakes with our three girls, but are thankful they can live in a loving home with parents who support them. So many are living without a family to love and protect them. If God hadn't done such an amazing work in my life, Rosella could still be in that situation.

I believe God saved me because He loves me and wanted a relationship with me, but I also believe He wanted to raise me up to be a godly man and father who will impact this broken world. Every believer should live with the understanding that they haven't just been saved for themselves. There is so much to be done for His glory and the sake of the multitudes of lost souls living all around us. We don't have to look very far to find people who need the Gospel and our help. Sometimes these individuals even have a way of finding us.

"Hello."

"Mr. Lindstrom?"

"Yes, this is Jed Lindstrom."

"This is the Texas Department of Children and Family Services."

With one phone call, life would never be the same again for any of us. The State of Texas wanted to know if Erica and I would consider adopting three of Rosella's siblings. There was never any question or hesitation. We just knew. Sometimes you just know when God is calling you to do something. The way we saw it, Rosella was only the beginning. She has a destiny in God and so do her brothers and sisters. If the Lord would offer the opportunity, grace, and provision to make ours a family of eight, who were we to stand in the way? The only thing left to do was walk through the open door and trust Him.

Be very careful, then, how you live—not as unwise but as wise, making the most of every opportunity, because the days are evil. Ephesians 5:15-16

Trusting God was of critical importance throughout the year-long process to bring the rest of the kids into our home. Friends poured out their prayers and financial support to see us through the battle that ensued. My sordid past did not make it an easy process. Understandably, felons cannot typically adopt children, so my first application was denied. I submitted all of the evidence I could to show the state that I was past my criminal behavior and was suitable to adopt. We won our appeal, and in September of 2016, we welcomed two boys and one more girl into our home, forming *TheLindstrom8*.

My greatest mistake in life was leaving Rosella behind as a baby, but God redeemed this horrible decision. It's mind boggling to think that he worked with the mess I made and not only restored my daughter to me, He opened up a home for all four of these siblings. Only the Lord does such personal and special miracles.

He restores. He gives second chances. He returns to us things that we have cast aside as nothing. Not because we deserve it; He does it because He loves to renew and redeem. When it seems like there is no way, even still He finds one.

TheLindstrom8 in November of 2016

Chapter 15

THE UNLIKELY ONES

"So that's my story," I said, trying to wrap up a testimony that could go on for hours, "the short version anyways."

He leaned back in his seat and said, "That's one hell of a story."

"You see, it's really a story about the miracles God did in my life even though I didn't deserve them. He calls me His beloved son and tells me He is pleased with me. God has always been looking out for me. The issue was that I wasn't looking for Him.

"A wise man once asked me, 'Jed, if there was someone who knew everything about you and still loved you, would you want to get to know this person? There is and His name is Jesus; He truly loves you.'

'I'm sure He does,' I confessed to the man, 'I've heard a lot about Him from people, but I've never personally experienced His love or presence in a way that made me want to give my life to Him.'

"This man prayed with me to surrender my life to Jesus, and although I did, it wasn't until five years later that I began to really live out that commitment."

With the hum of cars zipping around the track and the sounds of a largely intoxicated crowd as our backdrop, the man in our ministry tent proceeded to tell me his own story of God looking out for him.

"I almost died last night," he said as he pointed out the hospital bracelet still around his wrist, "from an overdose and alcohol poisoning. They had to revive me from the dead."

"Wow," was all I could manage to get out.

He looked up at me with desperate eyes, almost as if he was about to take his last breath. "I want help. I just want to stop ruining my life. I've known about God in the past, but never knew His presence or voice like you."

"It's not hard to hear His voice, but you have to listen."

Gripping his hand, I stopped talking and started praying. The Holy Spirit took over right away and it was evident He was impacting this man's heart. Scratched, bruised, and grungy from head to toe, he surrendered his life to Jesus right there at the DAYTONA® 500.

Some may say this man was an unlikely convert, but I think

he fit the bill perfectly. Whether it's been a drug addict, a Wall Street guru, or a Colombian orphan who gave their life to Christ, they have all shared a quiet desperation for hope and truth. In reality, we're all *unlikely* converts. We are without hope in this world unless the Lord reaches out to us. Hear the words of Jesus:

> *For no one can come to me unless the Father who sent me draws them to me, and at the last day I will raise them up.* John 6:44

Can you sense the Father drawing you today? Will you turn from your sin and trust Him to reveal His redemptive power and love to you? You desperately need a Savior; you cannot save yourself. No one can.

I am a living testimony of that power and love. No matter how many drugs I took or crimes I committed, there was never a moment in my life where God stopped loving me. More than ten years after falling to my knees in that jail cell, I still live out of the goodness of God. I watch Him work miracles every day. I'm not ashamed to share what He has done in me. He still saves today. He still heals today. He still loves you today regardless of what you have done.

We may think that we have it all together, that we have all the answers, or that we know what is best for us. We don't. His plan is always higher than ours. Always. Through prayer and time in His presence, I can hear His voice and know His plans as He reveals them to me step by step. He speaks clearly and moves in great power. There is nothing too hard for God. When He makes a promise, He keeps it. You can trust Him.

If someone knew everything about you and still loved you beyond anything you've known before, how close would you want to get to this person? If they offered to remove all of the guilt from your past and all of the stains from your sins, would you take them up on it?

If you've wavered on your answer, stop and consider that this life is a vapor. It will be over in the blink of an eye. Can you face an eternity separated from God? Can you even face another day of your life here on earth separated from Him? Why would you want to live another moment without Him?

Today is your day of salvation! Today is your day of healing and deliverance! Will you fully surrender your life to Jesus now?

HELPFUL SCRIPTURES

John 3:16-18

"For this is how God loved the world: He gave his one and only Son, so that everyone who believes in him will not perish but have eternal life. God sent his Son into the world not to judge the world, but to save the world through him. "There is no judgment against anyone who believes in him. But anyone who does not believe in him has already been judged for not believing in God's one and only Son.

Romans 3:23

For everyone has sinned; we all fall short of God's glorious standard.

Matthew 3:2

"Repent of your sins and turn to God, for the Kingdom of Heaven is near."

Acts 3:17-20

"Friends, I realize that what you and your leaders did to Jesus was done in ignorance. But God was fulfilling what all the prophets had foretold about the Messiah—that he must suffer these things. Now repent of your sins and turn to God, so that your sins may be wiped away. Then times of refreshment will come from the presence of the Lord, and he will again send you Jesus, your appointed Messiah.

John 10:10

The thief's purpose is to steal and kill and destroy. My purpose is to give them a rich and satisfying life.

2 Corinthians 5:18

"...and all of this is a gift from God, who brought us back to himself through Christ. And God has given us this task of reconciling people to him."

Malachi 4:6
"His preaching will turn the hearts of fathers to their children, and the hearts of children to their fathers. Otherwise I will come and strike the land with a curse."

Psalm 68:4-6
"Sing praises to God and to His name! Sing loud praises to His who rides on the clouds. His name id the Lord – rejoice in His presence! Father to the Fatherless, defender of widows –this is God, whose dwelling is holy."

Romans 12:1
"...and so dear brothers and sisters, I plead with you to give your bodies to God because of all He has done for you. Let them be a living and holy sacrifice – the kind He will find acceptable."

Matthew 6:10
May your Kingdom come soon. May your will be done on earth, as it is in heaven.

Matthew 6:33-34
Seek the Kingdom of God above all else, and live righteously, and he will give you everything you need. "So don't worry about tomorrow, for tomorrow will bring its own worries. Today's trouble is enough for today.

Ephesians 1:5
God decided in advance to adopt us into his own family by bringing us to himself through Jesus Christ. This is what he wanted to do, and it gave him great pleasure.

RESPOND TO GOD'S CALL

God has been good to me. In this book, I only scratched the surface of His marvelous blessings during my walk with Him. I thought I'd die a lying, thieving, worthless, drug-addicted criminal. I told God many times that I was sorry. I never meant it until October 11, 2004.

I remember God saying, "Jed, I forgive you. I cleanse you by the blood of my Son."

He will say the same thing to you when you turn from your sins and fully surrender to Him. Go to Him as you are. You don't need to get cleaned up to go to church. Go to church and get cleaned up. Watch Him work a miracle in your life.

I encourage you to not wait another day. I encourage you to live for Him with no reservations. Yes, have godly boundaries, but live courageously for Him. You will be part of His plan for this time and declare His wonderful handiwork.

I wrote this book because I believed God has called you into deeper intimacy with Him. He wants you to tell people about what led you to repentance. When you fully surrender your life to Jesus, you will know. He will reveal Himself to you. I suggest you write the date and time somewhere in this book so you can share that experience with others.

A simple plan for a healthy balance in life has helped me in my walk with the Lord. Either use these quick steps to begin your walk or use them to strengthen your walk. More information about each step can be found on our website www.letsgoministry.com.

SEVEN BASIC STEPS TO FOLLOW JESUS

1. Examine your life

Receiving eternal life is powerful and God will radically change your heart and life from this point on. As you open your heart to the Holy Spirit, examine yourself. You will fall deeper in love with God and know His heart more clearly.

2. Surround yourself with healthy support

You need others around you who can speak into your life. Submit yourself to a local life-giving, Holy Spirit-filled church. When you find one, introduce yourself to the pastor or leader, share with them how you have fully surrendered your life to Jesus, and tell them you want to know how to grow in your relationship with God. Don't go to church and hide.

3. Take care of your body

You may have some life-controlling habits, possibly drug addiction, pornography, poor eating habits, or laziness. Whatever it may be, that habit affects your body and spirit. Look at your habits and ask God if He wants you to change them. Don't fight His answer. The more time you spend with Him, the clearer you will hear Him. This is really a call to personal holiness, intimacy with God, and right living.

4. Accountability and discipleship

Find one or two mature believers who can walk with you as a mentor and hold you accountable as you grow in God. Someone willing to walk with you through the ups and downs of life. As you grow with the Lord, ask Him to send you someone you can be a mentor to, and disciple them in the word of God and encourage them in their new walk with Jesus.

5. Personal prayer life

Prayer is a responsibility and an honor. Seek God in every situation and opportunity so you can know His will clearly. Your personal prayer life also will lead you to times of fasting and corporate prayer with others for families, cities, and nations. Don't be afraid to pour out your heart to God in your language, using your own words. Make a list if one will help.

6. Be baptized in water and the Holy Spirit

You need the power of God in every circumstance. Being baptized in water is a public declaration of your allegiance to Him. But you also need the power of the Holy Spirit. When baptized in the Holy Spirit, you will pray in the Holy Spirit, meaning new tongues will be uttered as you pray and God will reveal the interpretation to you or another person.

7. Go with confidence and in love with God

Share your great news with others; with as many people as you can. Tell them about what Jesus has done, and is doing, in your life. Don't be shy. In the streets, in the jails, in the marketplaces —wherever God sends you, go, in the power of the Holy Spirit and in the love of God. Let Him use you for His glory. Let Jesus manifest His life through yours and radically change the environment wherever you go. You cannot turn this life with Jesus on and off as you desire. Always burn hot for Jesus.

I am a personal witness to the miraculous works of Jesus Christ. By the power of the Holy Spirit, bodies are made whole; the demon-possessed are set free and placed in their right mind; the lost are saved, brought to eternal life, and hope; and the lame walk and the deaf hear.

In the Bible, we read about God's desire for His kingdom to touch the earth so He can change whatever or whomever He touches. That could be you. That should be you. I believe God will use this book to inspire you to live for Jesus and follow Him all the days of your life.

God did a great work in me. He can do the same kind of great work in you when you are ready to break out.

ABOUT LETS GO MINISTRY

Evangelist Jed Lindstrom is the founder and director of Lets Go Ministry (LGM), an independent evangelistic ministry that seeks to bring transformation to individuals and communities through the power of the Gospel.

The mission of Lets Go Ministry is to boldly, creatively and compassionately bring the message of Jesus Christ to the lost and equip believers to do the same in their everyday lives. We accomplish our mission in three main ways.

Outreach: doing local outreach and short-term missions in the U.S. and abroad, as well as ministry in recovery centers, jails, prisons, and special events.

Exhortation: speaking at churches, ministries, and meetings of Christian leaders in order to encourage believers to share Christ.

Training: holding Messenger Training creative evangelism workshops and conferences in the U.S. and abroad.

INVITE JED TO SPEAK

- Jails, prisons, treatment centers
- Conferences, fundraisers or church events
- Bible schools, colleges, or discipleship programs
- Public schools that would allow a faith-based testimony
- Or give us your idea!

To schedule Jed to speak, visit us on the web at www.letsgoministry.com or www.jedsbook.com

Messenger Training is an invitation to the local church body to come and be equipped to partner with the Holy Spirit in living out the Great Commission. Lets Go Ministry's desire is to see ordinary men, women and children develop a passion for reaching the lost and the knowledge they need to be effective witnesses for Christ. The end goal is to see these witnesses released into a lifestyle of evangelism and for ongoing, thriving local church outreaches to be established.

We offer 1-day workshop and 2-day or 3-day conference formats, all taking place over weekends. These creative evangelism trainings combine all of the elements that we believe are vital to living a life of outreach: worship, intercession, teaching (scripture) and hands on practice.

Lets Go Ministry partners with churches to hold these trainings. Jed Lindstrom is willing to travel anywhere in the United States and abroad as he is able to lead Messenger Training conferences. He would love an opportunity to work with your church or ministry to bring this vibrant, hands on training to your city and help you to establish ongoing outreach in your community.

For more information on Messenger Training
visit us on the web at www.messengertraining247.com
or email us at info@letsgoministry.com.

FROM THE DESK OF RUSSELL HOLLOWAY

I first traveled with Jed Lindstrom to New York City in July 2011. We encouraged hard-working pastors who labored around the city. We fed the homeless. We prayed with dozens of people outside a Starbucks® in the Wall Street area of Lower Manhattan. Many times I witnessed the power of Jed's personal testimony.

His life story isn't just for the lost, or the poor, or the addict. His story resonates with anyone who is open to Jesus' message of love and redemption.

I ask that you support Jed and Lets Go Ministry. My wife and I want to provide free books to as many people as possible. Please prayerfully consider joining us in supporting Jed's efforts to go into the "no go places" with the saving message of Jesus.

God has been and will be glorified for years to come by Jed's story and message. Let's all work together to lift up the name of Jesus.

Russell Holloway, MS, LMHC, NCC
Director of Counseling Services, Port Orange Counseling Center,
Ormond Beach Counseling Center, and
Daytona Beach Marriage Center

ORDER MORE BOOKS

Order more books today for your ministry, organization, or to give to others.

Donate Books: You can purchase books for Lets Go Ministry to freely give to others who are in need of hearing a story of hope and restoration. This is not tax deductible, but allows the ministry to help others!

Bulk Order Discounts: Shipments are available of 50+ books at a time. If you are interested in buying bulk, contact us at www.jedsbook.com.

Give as a Gift: *Break Out* makes a great gift for others in your life.

Purchase Books to Sell at Your Store: The book is available for you to sell at your church or store.

Small Group Study: You may also order books as part of a small group or Bible study.

Find out more at www.jedsbook.com

Visit Us On The Web